Fit to Bust
How great companies fail

TIM PHILLIPS

KoganPage

LONDON PHILADELPHIA NEW DELHI

First published in Great Britain and the United States in 2011 by Kogan Page Limited

120 Pentonville Road	1518 Walnut Street, Suite 1100	4737/23 Ansari Road
London N1 9JN	Philadelphia PA 19102	Daryaganj
United Kingdom	USA	New Delhi 110002
www.koganpage.com		India

© Tim Phillips, 2011

The right of Tim Phillips to be identified as the author of this work has been asserted by him in accordance with the Copyright, Designs and Patents Act 1988.

ISBN 978 0 7494 6013 6
E-ISBN 978 0 7494 6014 3

British Library Cataloguing-in-Publication Data
A CIP record for this book is available from the British Library.

Library of Congress Cataloging-in-Publication Data
Phillips, Tim, 1967-
    Fit to bust : how great companies fail / Tim Phillips.
        p. cm.
    Includes bibliographical references.
    ISBN 978-0-7494-6013-6 – ISBN 978-0-7494-6014-3 (ebook) 1. Business failures. 2. Management.
3. Business failures–Case studies. 4. Management–Case studies. I. Title.
    HG3761.P47 2011
    658.1'6–dc22
                                010048641

Typeset by Saxon Graphics Ltd, Derby
Production managed by Jellyfish
Printed and bound in the UK by CPI Antony Rowe

Contents

05   All together now 89

06   Greater fools 115

07   Look what we made 137

08   Almost revolutionary 163

Acknowledgements

I was planning to write this book a couple of years ago, but then companies kept failing. I suppose I should be grateful.

Thank you Alyssa Danigelis and Professor Bonnie Fox Garrity for doing valuable research that I would have missed. Also Professor Patricia Hutton of Canisius College in Buffalo, NY. Apparently if you're planning a book and you mention it to her in conversation, she can organize a seminar on the subject where other people will give you lots of good ideas that you never would have thought of yourself. That's my experience, anyway.

My agent Rob Dudley and my editor Jon Finch were extraordinarily polite about trifling things like missed deadlines.

Finally my wife Nazaret. Good news Naza: at the end of this sentence, I've finished.

Chapter One
Bad Behaviour

By any standards, 2009 was a difficult year for large companies. Of the Fortune 500 list, 128 of the companies made a loss in 2009. That compares with 66 in 2004 and 67 in 1999. Finding big companies to go bust is an entertaining reverse stock-picking game, but not as tough as it has been in recent history.

In April 2009, the website 24/7 Wall St. published a list of 10 brands that would disappear or be acquired by the end of 2010. The carnage was so swift that, in December 2009, it published another list. And, in June 2010, a third list.[1]

In each list, more than half of the predictions came true. Many of the companies that limped through survived through desperate and savage cost-cutting. Brands that had been widely admired a few years previously – GM or Sun Microsystems for example – had failed to survive independently.

There will always be business failures – without the possibility of failure, there isn't the possibility that exciting or innovative new companies will become successful. Analysts and the business press exist because we need to track the trajectory of these meteors. Financial services backs the winners and withdraws support from the losers.

But when we look at who fails, when, and how, it's often shocking how far and how fast great companies can fall. After the event we can spot the problems, but a common theme in this book is the adulation that many failures bask in, right until the last moment. Afterwards we credit the small group of contrarians who were the first to spot a major failure, and rightly so. Yet in the four centuries that this book covers, we haven't become appreciably better at resisting bubbles, spotting charlatans or maintaining momentum.

One of the most important business books of the past 20 years was *Built to Last*, by Jim Collins and Jerry Porras. The authors asked 65 large company CEOs which companies they considered to be the most visionary, and why. As a result, they compiled a list of 18 companies that not only dominated their markets, but which would do so in a consistent, long-lasting way.

Published in 2004, the book inspired thousands of leaders. It's a terrific read. But as the magazine *Fast Company*[2] pointed out on the tenth anniversary of its publication – by which time the book had sold 3.5 million copies and been translated into 16 languages – its ability to inspire was better than its ability to predict which companies were 'built to last': 'The fact remains that at least 7 of BTL's original 18 companies have stumbled… scarcely better than the results you'd get by flipping a coin.'

The tenth anniversary article interviewed the authors, and other academics, on how effectively we can say that any organization is built to last in the long term. 'For the most part, my experience has been that people haven't gotten hung up on the list of companies. At least intelligent, practicing leaders haven't gotten hung up on it', Collins says. In 2009, he published a further book – based on long-term research – on how companies that are built to last forget their values.

There is, however, the argument that Collins and Porras produced a wonderful and insightful book on how some managers and some companies can improve their performance, which has inspired a generation of high-achieving managers to do mostly positive things for themselves, their department, their branch office or – occasionally – their company (when you sell millions of copies, they don't all get bought by the CEO). And yet, when you copy the habits of the successful companies in the book, you are no more 'built to last' than they are. There are bigger forces at work here.

Stuff happens

When a British prime minister was asked by a journalist what factors were most likely to blow a company off course, he answered: 'Events, dear boy, events.'[3]

Asking what causes all companies to fail is a bit like asking what is the best colour to paint a work of art so that it will sell. There's plenty of historical data, and I'm sure that we can make a correlation between colours and auction prices, especially if we select a small group of paintings, and look for what they have in common.

What really makes great companies succeed or fail? Events, internal and external.

Collins and Porras know this very well: Collins says that the most important part of the book is chapter four: 'Preserve the core! And! Stimulate progress! To be built to last, you have to be built for change!' Ceaseless innovation has been at the heart of what made some companies great: Google, Dyson or Apple, for example. As we will see, it has also made some companies into a mess.

Richard D'Aveni, professor of strategic management at Dartmouth's Tuck School of Business, is one of the critics of business books in general. They give a set of instructions that make people feel terrific about themselves, he says, but it creates activity rather than results:

> One, tell people what they want to hear and give them hope. Two, make it a Rorschach test [a test designed to show intelligence, personality and mental state, in which the subject interprets ink-blots, and three, keep it so simple that it really doesn't examine the truth of the world in enough depth so people get a false sense of clarity.[4]

Maybe that activity is the point – an energetic group, whatever its method, is more likely to correct faults. But, as we will also see, it has created a cult of management, where we pursue destructive strategies until they drive the business into the ground because they must be correct, or where we blindly follow a charismatic leader to destruction, because the leader has told us it's the best thing to do.

The stuff that happens might be a global financial crisis; if it weren't for a very particular set of events, then Lehman Brothers or AIG would have continued on their path, at least in the short term, creating extraordinary profits for a little longer. It might be a simple exhaustion of the market available – the most extreme examples of which cause Ponzi schemes inevitably to fail, and pyramid marketing to run out of steam.

It might be a single, disastrous decision that undermines years of hard work. It might be overreach, an attempt to change the world in a way that the world doesn't want to be changed, or an attempt to expand that takes two great companies and produces a single mediocre one.

Can we build to last?

We have a problem: the same superficial features of success are also the telltales of failure. It suggests that it's not what you do, but how you do it, that counts.

Bob Sutton, a professor of management science and engineering at Stanford Engineering School, published a manifesto in 2006 called 'Management Advice: Which 90 per cent is Crap?' Despite having been twice included in Harvard Business School's yearly list of 'Breakthrough Business Ideas', he admitted that 'I've never actually seen a new idea on their list... I confess that none of our ideas were new, let alone a breakthrough.'[5] He points us to advice he received from his colleague, and organizational theorist, James March: 'Most claims of originality are testimony to ignorance and most claims of magic are testimony to hubris.'

So why are we so in love with the idea that great management is the product of great ideas? Sutton has two explanations: the first is that we create a narrative for the project (he uses mergers as an example). It becomes the job of a lot of people to sell this as a very good idea. Not just people inside the company, but the advisers, consultants, business book writers, and other assorted hangers-on. When it succeeds, we decide that this, pseudo-scientifically, provides proof of concept. It might do nothing of the sort, of course. It might provide evidence of something else. It might have been blind luck and good timing. Companies have a lot of moving parts. 'Psychological research suggests that many others have actually convinced themselves to believe their own lousy logic and arguments. Human beings see what they believe, and disregard the rest.'

If you're a ship's captain and there are icebergs in the sea, your grand strategy for avoiding icebergs is of secondary importance as soon as you cast off. What matters to your passengers is that, when you're approaching an iceberg, you spot what's happening and change course. The companies and investors in this book didn't. Why not?

In Chapter 2, the companies looked at the iceberg, and thought they could plough right through it if they told people it was smaller than it looked.

In Chapter 3, the companies had avoided some small icebergs, so they sailed full steam ahead at the biggest one they could find.

In Chapter 4, the captain said the iceberg didn't exist, and we believed him (it's usually a him in this case).

In Chapter 5, we all agreed that, even if there was an iceberg, it was probably better to keep going straight ahead.

By Chapter 6, we raced each other to see who could hit the iceberg first.

In Chapter 7, the captains are so busy squabbling that they don't even see the iceberg.

And finally, in Chapter 8, we meet the people who thought they had built a magic boat.

A word on classification

Business failure is a mess. People blame each other, save themselves, shred documents, try hare-brained attempts to save the company, sell chunks, spin off brands. Sometimes they even get billions of dollars or government backing to bail them out. Smart CEOs, looking for someone to forgive them, create their own narrative in which other people are to blame.

This has two consequences. The first is that you could take many of these companies and drop them into a different chapter, simply by emphasizing a different crazy thing they did. If you have a charismatic leader who bets the company on a sausage ice-cream franchise, is that a failure of leadership or innovation?

The second is that there are so many companies to include that it's impossible to cover them all. There are some basket cases that didn't make it in for reasons of space, or simply because they are just a horrible, depressing mess. Others have snuck in because, while as companies they were insignificant or ephemeral, they're extremely entertaining. Though not, we must add, for the employees or the shareholders.

And that's the final point: we love success. This book is about the obsessive desire for success, based on our desire to think well of ourselves; and how that destroys good companies. In the abstract that's the price we are prepared to pay. Our pensions depend on stock-pickers who get some right, some wrong, but who maintain a decent average.

On the other hand, business failure represents lives ruined, jobs lost, communities destroyed, time and money wasted for real people – many of whom couldn't do anything about it. This book won't tell you how to get rich (actually, none of the books that claim they do actually do. If they did, do you think the authors would write a book about it?), but it might help you spot a disaster if you are willing to look critically at the companies you work for, invest in or buy from.

Machiavelli wrote one of the first business books, and one of the best, when he wrote *The Prince* in 1513.[6] I'm not recommending you follow his advice to the letter. Today, any manager who uses Machiavelli's idea of cutting your enemy in half and leaving him in the town square as a memo to all staff about loyalty might end up in an HR seminar, at least.

Machiavelli wrote *The Prince* because he was frustrated by the egonomics in other leadership manuals that were around at the time. He considered them soft-headed. They all recycled the same information: that successful Princes were fair, gentle, educated and positive. Machiavelli, however, had spent his career working for these princes, and he knew that the books were just written to make the Princes feel good about themselves: the Rorschach test that Professor D'Aveni refers to.

Problem is, when you write something that's more honest, you don't make friends. The Prince did for Machiavelli's career as a political fixer, partly because it was too honest about what it took to be an effective leader at that time, and partly because he didn't espouse the idea that renaissance principalities were Built To Last. It's not surprising that he couldn't get a job when he was telling the local aristocracy not to get too comfortable on the throne:

> One sees a ruler flourishing today and ruined tomorrow, without his having changed at all in character or qualities... we are successful when our ways are suited to the time and circumstances, and unsuccessful when they are not... Two men, acting differently, may achieve the same results; and if two men act the same way, one might succeed and the other fail.

Which is a pretty depressing description of what's going on in the Fortune 500. On the other hand, for those of us who aren't within touching distance of those thrones, the history of how failure has been clutched from the jaws of success offers a collection of great stories.

I'd say that we might learn something but, if there's a takeaway from this, as business books say, then it's this: we don't know as much as we think we do.

Chapter Two
Too good to fail

> *It takes 20 years to build a reputation and five minutes to ruin it. If you think about that, you'll do things differently.*
> **WARREN BUFFETT**

Success in business means delivering results, and results are measured in money. We have never been more focused on how companies deliver their numbers. The numbers game has become spectacularly unforgiving – so much so that the need to deliver has pushed three of the most highly regarded innovators of the modern era over the edge.

Until almost the end, almost everyone considered them better than their peers at doing the things they did: it wasn't that they were too big to fail. They were too good to fail.

And, at one time, they probably were.

We have all felt the pressure to live up to expectations. For organizations like Enron and WorldCom, and for Bernard Madoff, satisfying unsustainable expectations became the business. It wasn't enough just to be better: they had to carry on being better, every quarter, forever.

No company wants to make the transition from exciting, high-growth market leader to dull, steady-state, low-growth also-ran. But making that transition successfully might just be the best chance for long-term survival for many companies. It rarely happens without some crisis, break-up or crushing period of disappointment, but happen it must.

The alternative, at least for these three, was to engage in an ever more frantic dance to maintain their carefully constructed illusion of genius. The companies that they built ended in ruins, along with the lives of investors and employees. Some of the people responsible ended in prison, but not all of them.

Satisfying expectations is a sophisticated game. So much so that, right up to almost the end, all three of these companies were fawned over by investors, analysts and press. The people who pointed to holes in the balance sheet and hail-Mary strategies that didn't make sense, so obvious after the event, tended to be either politely ignored or tolerated – very much in the way that we ignore the fact that someone has forgotten to zip his trousers. We look twice as hard in the other direction.

Actually, it's these companies that were like unzipped trousers: no matter how smart they were, it was only a matter of time before something unpleasant was exposed.

Isn't that meant to be $50 million?
Bernard Madoff

Bernard Madoff, then 71 years old, retired on 26 September 2009 when he was sentenced to spend 150 years in prison in North Carolina.[7]

Bernard L. Madoff Investment Securities, his $64.8 billion Ponzi scheme, had made Madoff a hero of the most sophisticated financial market in the world. He took deposits from investment funds with assets of billions, funds with staffs of compliance experts and risk managers, for more than two decades. His returns were impossible to sustain in the real world and his statements were riddled with errors. The one person who bothered to look closely published detailed exposés of Madoff's crimes, but was ignored.

How did Madoff pull it off?

He made it work because he promised, and delivered, big rates of return to investors. People clamoured to get into his scheme because of the success of those already in it. Madoff made them look successful – he was one of them.

Madoff was, until 2008, one of the great men of Wall Street – a former president of NASDAQ, a market maker (a bulk trader who helps to establish market prices by dealing in large volumes of shares) whose trading, at one point in the 1990s, accounted for 9 per cent of all the trades done on the New York Stock Exchange (NYSE).

The fictional Madoff miracle was a long time in creation: already a market maker, he started to invest in the 1960s on behalf of a few private clients. He promised them a return of 18 per cent on their investments, and he made good on his promise. Michael Bienes, of the firm of Avellino & Bienes in Fort Lauderdale, found investors for him among the rich and retired of Florida. 'It was like a money machine... people said to me, you must have worked very hard. I say, no, I didn't', he says now.[8] Bienes was the first of thousands not to ask questions, as long as the money kept coming. He admits now that he had no idea how Madoff could outperform the market so spectacularly, or explain it to his clients: 'How do you split an atom? I know you can split them, I don't know how you do it. How does an aeroplane fly?'

We can say with hindsight that you clients climbed into Madoff's aeroplane and then he pretended to make the ground disappear.

The ace money manager

By the 1990s, Madoff had around 3,200 clients. Only trouble was, he didn't even have a licence to invest on their behalf. It was then, 17 years before he was found out, that regulators first thought he must be running a Ponzi scheme, and first gave him a clean bill of health.

'Here's a tantalizing Wall Street mystery', the *Wall Street Journal* wrote on 16 December 1992. 'The Securities and Exchange Commission [SEC] recently cracked down on one of the largest-ever sales of unregistered securities... The pair had promised investors hard-to-believe annual returns of 13.5% to 20% – to be obtained by turning the money over to be managed by an unnamed broker. Regulators feared it all might be just a huge scam. "We went into this thinking it could be a major catastrophe," says Richard Walker, the SEC's New York regional administrator.'

Yet the money was there when they investigated: 'The mystery broker turns out to be none other than Bernard L. Madoff – a highly successful and controversial figure on Wall Street, but until now not known as an ace money manager.'

Madoff claimed the returns were nothing special, but they were way ahead of what most money managers were delivering. 'They took in nearly a half a billion dollars in customer money totally outside the system that we can monitor and regulate', says the SEC's Mr Walker. 'That's pretty frightening.'

Madoff was vague about his investment strategy, gave limited reports to investors about how the money was made, even during two years – 1984 and 1991 – when the stock market declined in value. The article treats this as an amusing piece of gossip:

> The 54-year-old Mr. Madoff says he didn't know the money he was managing had been raised illegally. And he insists the returns were really nothing special, given that the Standard & Poor's 500-stock index generated an average annual return of 16.3% between November 1982 and November 1992. 'I would be surprised if anybody thought that matching the S&P over 10 years was anything outstanding,' he says.

Speculation at the time suggested that Madoff's $440 million investment business and his market-making share dealing were linked. It would have been against the law, but 'front running' – putting your client purchases and sales through when you know that a large-scale trade, which will move the price, is about to happen – is commonplace.

Having had his knuckles rapped by the Securities and Exchange Commission, Madoff went on with his money management in a more formal capacity, but still with the same way of working: small brokers recruited for him, especially among the independently wealthy. Some of Europe's richest families turned over everything to him (his creditors include 17 funds in Luxembourg alone). The feeder funds paid 2 per cent commission, but got 1 per cent back if they helped recruit. The fund ballooned from $4 billion to $65 billion from 2000 to 2008.

The ace fraudster

At some point, Madoff abandoned trading almost completely in favour of fraud.

It is impossible to decipher when the reported returns of his business became detached from the real returns; we only know that they did long before 2009; hence the need to keep recruitment going. Gradually the stress of paying illusory returns on capital that had already been paid out created a sealed-off business, two floors below Madoff's market-making business. CFO Frank DiPascali, who had worked closely with Madoff for 33 years after being recruited by Madoff's secretary (who lived next door), fabricated statements for investors every month that were printed and mailed to them. DiPascali pleaded guilty to 10 counts of assisting fraud, admitting that he knew what was going on – but that he thought the money could one day be repaid. Madoff's auditor, David Friehling, pleaded guilty to filing false audit reports. Two more programmers also pleaded guilty.

Two floors up, nobody knew.

Yet any client who looked closely at a statement would have been able to spot mistakes: trades in companies that no longer existed, or apparent massive trades which didn't show up in that day's business. It was strange enough that the statements were printed on paper and mailed, long after rival money managers had switched to easy-to-check electronic statements. It was remarkable that a $65 billion business was in the hands of a few people – though they wouldn't have been overworked, we know now. Many of his funds made no trades at all.

It is most remarkable, though, that an out-of-town accountant could unmask the fraud in four hours in May 2000, deliver clear, factual, concise evidence of the scale of the crime to the SEC repeatedly – despite fearing for his safety

– and still be ignored. Harry Markopolos did not buy Madoff's 'show me the money' defence. In November 2005 he even sent a 21-page memo to the SEC titled: 'The World's Largest Hedge Fund is a Fraud', containing 29 red flags. When that was ignored he continued to provide evidence. At least seven other concerned citizens raised doubts. And yet the SEC's investigation was, at times, farcical. It compared faked documents provided by Madoff to other fake documents provided to investors, and found no discrepancies. When they found inconsistencies, junior investigators stayed silent.

Madoff made the most of the SEC's incompetence. Though he must have lived in fear that one investigator, at least, would break ranks to reveal the obvious, none did.

It allowed Madoff to claim to investors that the SEC had examined his books and found nothing. As long as the fund kept paying out, the concerned citizens were in the minority.

Markopolos had sent the following e-mail, one of many to the SEC, in June 2007: 'When Madoff finally does blow up, it's going to be spectacular.' It was.

The downfall

In December 2008, with the stock market in crisis, many investors needed to redeem funds. Faced with a bill for $7 billion in redemptions, Madoff knew the fraud was over. On 10 December his sons, Andrew and Mark, confronted their father. He confessed, saying he was 'absolutely finished', and had lost $50bn. The sons called a lawyer, who alerted the FBI and the SEC. According to the FT, one SEC official thought the scale of the fraud had accidentally been typed in 1,000 times too large: 'Isn't that number meant to be $50 million?' he asked.

Madoff has ruined the lives of thousands. He is directly responsible for at least one ruined investor committing suicide. On 11 December 2008 Madoff was courteously interviewed at home in his bathrobe and slippers by the FBI. Reportedly he told them that his investment business was 'One big lie'.

Many people who gave money to Madoff now admit they suspected that something wasn't right. When the fund crashed, the *Financial Times* reported a trustee from an educational institution (in the United States, universities often sit on huge investment funds, based on gifts from alumni): 'I thought he might be front-running or something dubious like that – I never would have thought he was just inventing the whole thing', he said.[9]

Effectively the trustee is saying: 'I thought he was stealing, just not as much.' Also the trustee thought that Madoff wasn't stealing from him, he was stealing for him, so he wasn't going to get outraged about that. With friends like this, Madoff was given enough rope to hang himself and all his clients. Like them, he sponsored dinners and golf tournaments and gave to charity.

There's an excuse that the SEC was overworked and understaffed. The SEC uses it. It's partly true, but that's not the end of the matter. It wasn't as if the SEC had to do very much work – it simply had to use evidence, rather than reputation, to guide whom it investigated. The SEC ignored the doubts about Madoff partly for the same reason that the investors didn't do due diligence or check their statements: he was innocent because he was rich and successful.

On 4 February 2009, in a testimony to the House Financial Services Subcommittee on Capital Markets, Insurance, and Government Sponsored Enterprises, Markopolos accused the SEC of being a captive of the industry it regulated. It continued to 'roar like a mouse and bite like a flea'.[10]

'I gift-wrapped and delivered the largest Ponzi scheme in history to [the SEC], and somehow they couldn't be bothered to conduct a proper investigation. I gave them a road map and a flashlight to find the fraud', he said. 'They haven't earned their pay checks and they need to be replaced.'

The meanest SOBs *WorldCom*

Think accountants are mild types? You never worked at WorldCom. At least Bernard Madoff used excellent manners when he was stealing from his clients.[11]

'If you show those damn numbers to the f*cking auditors, I'll throw you out the window',[12] was the reaction of Buddy Yates, director of WorldCom General Accounting, when one of his senior managers showed him the quarterly figures. And when internal auditors discovered that the figures the company reported bore little relation to reality, the chief financial officer (CFO) screamed at the auditor that she wasn't to tell the audit committee. Senior managers repeatedly bullied staff into lying about the state of Enron's accounts; when they said they didn't agree with the way the figures were being fixed, the managers fixed them anyway.

WorldCom Group, at one time the world's largest internet carrier, filed for Chapter 11 bankruptcy on 21 July 2002, a failure in financial terms which was even bigger than Enron's. Among the things that WorldCom did before it collapsed: it provided the computer networks for air traffic control in the United States; it ran the networks for the US Department of Defense and the General Accounting Office. It had $30 billion revenues, $104 billion of assets, and 60,000 employees. There was concern that, if the networks that WorldCom had acquired were turned off, the internet would simply grind to a halt.

Some of the other things that WorldCom did, in the words of Judge Jed Rakoff, who decided a 2003 civil case against WorldCom: 'We have perhaps the largest accounting fraud in history, with the company's income overstated by an estimated $11 billion, its balance sheet overstated by more than $75 billion, and the loss to shareholders estimated at as much as $200 billion.'

Two powerful, charismatic leaders at WorldCom simplified the fraud model that Enron pioneered. Where Enron's deceptions were complex, often on the borderline of legality, and an outgrowth of genuine innovation, WorldCom's desire to keep boosting its share price in a recession drew it into a culture of crude deceptions. Ten years later, it's hard to believe that a giant corporation could be captured by a cadre of fraudsters. Some stood back and did nothing. Others colluded. The board asked no questions.

At the top of WorldCom, Bernard Ebbers, known as Bernie, an ex-milkman, bartender, bouncer, car salesman, truck driver, factory foreman, basketball coach and hotelier, had built the company from a loss-making discount long-distance carrier into a global power. He wore sweatsuits to work and didn't use e-mail. He took over as chief executive officer (CEO) of LDDS – which was to become WorldCom – in 1984, not because he was an expert in telecoms, but because, he joked, he was 'the meanest SOB they could find'.

All over the place

He quickly made the company profitable. Immediately afterwards, he started to acquire other small telecoms carriers, and by 1993, LDDS was the fourth-largest long-distance carrier. It changed its name to WorldCom in 1995, and a year later US law was changed so that long-distance carriers were permitted to enter the local services market: WorldCom made another acquisition, a group called MFS Communications Company Inc., which cost $12.4 billion – and gave WorldCom a large internet backbone. In 1997, it made its biggest acquisition, buying competitor MCI for $42 billion. WorldCom made 60 acquisitions while it was growing.

On one hand, the mergers bought scale. But the company's structure was literally all over the place. A former accountant at the company told the US government's investigation into WorldCom that: 'We had offices in places we never knew about. We'd get calls from people we didn't even know existed.' In the rush to grow the share price, the accounting systems of many acquisitions were never merged.

Growth by acquisition could not go on indefinitely: in 2000, a projected merger with US carrier Sprint was blocked by regulators. There would be no more big acquisitions for WorldCom, and so it had to find ways to keep driving growth through performance. Already, though, that was a problem. The dotcom bubble was bursting, and prices and margins were declining radically. Many of its smaller competitors had gone out of business, which meant that the few carriers who needed to buy telecoms networks to compete with WorldCom could purchase them cheaply. The future did not look bright.

And so some of WorldCom's executives created an alternative reality through accounting. Carrier revenues are notoriously complex: when you make a phone call or send data, it has to pass through the networks of many carriers in many countries. Each time the carrier uses someone else's capacity, it must pay for it, and vice versa. Carriers own some of their network, but lease other parts.

The financial position of a carrier is, effectively, a best guess: a snapshot of the cash coming in and going out. With many types of business, and many types of accounting software, it was possible to distort the picture at WorldCom. It's part of a CFO's job to make the numbers look good using what are known as GAAP – generally accepted accounting principles. GAAP isn't totally rigid, because accountancy needs to be interpretive. GAAP is structured as rules which trust auditors to use it responsibly, because it allows for some interpretation of the facts. It allows the company to adjust how it treats some of the money in and money out, because a telecommunications company is not a fast food restaurant.

This is a good thing for complex companies in an ideal world, because it allows their accountants to paint a picture of what's actually happening – rather than just type some figures into a box, leaving us to make sense of it.

Another world

WorldCom thought a long way outside that box. It took GAAP apart and started to create its own reality, starting in 1998. The largest part of the fraud was simple but lucrative. The company estimated line costs every month for the calls its customers made. The bills would be settled with other carriers three months later, but meanwhile WorldCom had to estimate those costs, and match them against the revenues they had already received from customers. WorldCom had, in the language of accountants, a liability accrual: money that it would owe when it paid its phone bill. The accrual was subtracted from profits.

Sometimes the estimate would be too high: the phone bill was lower than expected, and WorldCom's earnings would be boosted by the difference. By 1999, Scott Sullivan, WorldCom's CFO (and *CFO Magazine*'s 'CFO Excellence' award winner in 1998), was directing business units to systematically lower the estimates. The effect was to boost WorldCom's earnings without changing the amount of business it was doing.

The methods used to do this were, at best, heavy-handed persuasion, and at worst, outright bullying. 'I guess the only way I am going to get this booked is to fly to DC and book it myself', senior vice president and controller David Myers told the head of one of the business units who had been brave enough to refuse to change his numbers for no reason other than that the CFO wanted them changed. When he still declined to cook the books, the staff at the general accounting department did it for him – presumably saving Myers the air fare.

The accruals were not loose change: one incident involved releasing $370 million, which the director of the business unit refused, on the simple basis that there was no reason to downgrade the accrual. So Betty Vinson, a senior manager who worked in general accounting, obtained the account number behind the director's back, and told one of her staff to make the change.

In less than two years WorldCom released $3.3 billion of accruals in this way. The problem: they made the results look good, but when the bills came in, those bills had to be settled. The sums put aside in the accounts were not even close to the true size of the bills. The company's performance on paper was swiftly losing any resemblance to its real financial status.

When there were no more accruals to massage, Sullivan switched to plan B. Many of the accounting frauds in this book are sophisticated and hard to understand or explain. WorldCom's is not in that category. As Karen Nelson, a professor of accounting at Stanford School of Business, commented at the time: 'What WorldCom did wrong is something that's taught in the first few weeks of a core financial reporting class. That's why people are asking, given its basic nature and magnitude, how it could have been missed.'

After years of growth, the company had a lot of network. The internet, as former United States Senator Ted Stevens memorably described it, is a 'system of tubes',[13] and WorldCom had leased, or acquired leases for, a lot of those tubes. Far more than it needed: there was a recession on, and following a glut of network-building in the dotcom boom, there was far too much capacity, and no buyers.

WorldCom had a lot of unused capacity that it had to pay for, because there were heavy financial penalties for breaking a lease. This is an operating cost. You need to pay every month to keep the assets that you don't need.

The wheeze that senior management dreamed up (Ebbers claimed that he didn't know the details: he was a salesman, he later told investigators, not an accountant) was to treat the cost of the leases as capital expenditure, as if the company had bought a new machine which would be profitable when it was switched on. So $771 million of unused capacity was moved to become 'construction in progress' in April 2001 to cover worse-than-expected revenues, which meant that it could be recognized as an asset. The assets were spread across five different accounts to make them harder to trace.

WorldCom escaped censure from its auditors Arthur Andersen who, according to the report prepared by the board afterwards, were by that time taking the figures presented by the many confusing parts of WorldCom on trust. The auditor examined whether they fitted expectations at a high level. It was not checking where those figures came from, as it had originally done. Accountants inside the company were leaned on heavily to make the numbers look good: Vinson, who was later sentenced to a jail term for her part in the fraud, later admitted that she complied partly because she was scared to lose her job in a recession. She trusted the CFO. He was widely admired: just as many carriers were making losses, WorldCom's numbers seemed to defy gravity.

WorldCom's fraud was eventually exposed not by shareholders (who were enjoying the ride far too much to look closely – not forgetting that many of them worked for the company), not by the external auditors, who were taking far too much on trust, and not by analysts, who were blinded by the reputation that Ebbers had massaged of being some kind of corporate superman. At the beginning of 2002, the only major suspicion about WorldCom came from its own internal audit team, 24 people under the control of Cynthia Cooper. When the ream found discrepancies in the accounts, the auditors were at first blocked, then warned. Sullivan screamed at Cooper after she raised the problems to WorldCom's audit committee. Stay away from this, he told her.

A systemic attitude

By this time the Securities and Exchange Commission was also curious about WorldCom's incredible numbers, and was asking for more information.

Cooper became the latest WorldCom employee to break the rules: by going behind her boss's back to get to the heart of the problem. She worked secretly, after hours, digging into the financial data, with her co-worker Gene Morse.

Soon after the SEC's request, the game was up. The board, which had taken little interest in the day-to-day running of the company, was staffed with industry veterans, but more than half were outside directors. They attended short, infrequent meetings at which they listened to presentations. They had no day-to-day contact with the chief officers. It had loaned Ebbers $400 million, because he had invested in outside businesses using his shares as collateral, and the value of the stock had declined. By 26 April, even the board knew something was up. It asked Ebbers to resign, promising him $1.5 million a year for life. His loans were restructured, so he didn't have to sell his rice farm or his hockey team.

With Ebbers gone, the audit team could work faster, and discovered $3 billion in questionable expenses by June 2002. By 25 June, the directors were forced to admit that it had inflated its profits by $3.8 billion – a figure that, with hindsight, was far too low. The next day, the SEC launched a lawsuit against WorldCom for civil fraud, which was later settled.

WorldCom eventually emerged from this mess, minus 17,000 employees, with the name of MCI – one of the many companies it swallowed on the way up. This was shortly after the board of directors' special investigators had concluded in their report that there had been 'a systemic attitude conveyed from the top down that employees should not question their superiors, but simply do what they were told'.

At MCI, things would be different. Every employee had to complete an ethics CD ROM, voiced by 'Karen': 'Imagine a restaurant with an open kitchen – where patrons have a clear view of a spotless kitchen. The restaurant invites inspection not only to reassure diners about the kitchen's cleanliness, but also to showcase their high standards', she told employees. 'If a violation is suspected, you must take appropriate steps to address the matter immediately. Failure to meet these standards may result in termination of employment.'

MCI was bought by Verizon in 2005. In 2007, Ebbers was sentenced to 25 years in prison for fraud, conspiracy and filing false documents, of which he will serve at least 85 per cent. He refused to admit his guilt, and cried in court. Sullivan, his CFO, did admit fraud and conspiracy, saying that he did it only to try to keep WorldCom going. He admitted his decisions had been 'cowardly'. His home was sold to pay creditors. He helped the government prosecute Ebbers.

'WorldCom could not have failed as a result of the actions of a limited number of individuals', said Richard Thornburgh, former US Attorney General, who was part of the investigation and prosecution. 'Rather, there was a total breakdown of the system of internal controls, corporate governance and individual responsibility.'

Even after completing their ethics CD ROM, many remaining employees resented Cooper, not Ebbers, for destroying the value of their shareholding or their pension plan. Like many organizations dominated by a charismatic cult, a destructive and criminal pattern of behaviour had become normal; the whistleblower became the traitor.

Ethics trainer Karen told employees that: 'At MCI, we now share a renewed commitment to the highest levels of integrity and transparency in the way we do business.' But Cooper recalls that nobody at WorldCom ever said 'thank you' to her for cleaning up WorldCom's kitchen. She didn't even get a promotion, and quit in 2004.

Ask why *Enron*

When Jeff Skilling, the former Enron president and CEO, was convicted on 19 counts and sentenced to 24 years in prison, the headline of the *Houston Chronicle* read 'Guilty! Guilty!'[14]

But what was Skilling, and Enron, guilty of?

Enron's advertising used to show three blind mice, walking with sticks and guide dogs through an office, representing those of us unlucky enough to do business without the benefit of its expertise.[15] Yet rather than providing clarity for its investors, Enron hid behind financial engineering a balance-sheet manipulation, and – remarkably – sustained the lie for several years.

In its increasingly wild attempts to keep growing and prove that it wasn't just better than its competition – but cleverer than every other company in history – Enron took its collective genius and used it to lie, cheat and defraud. If there's a narrative of how being paid in cash and adulation for your excellence can corrupt you, then Enron's 2001 collapse is that story.

Changing everything

'People who have really creative ideas are people who keep asking, "why?".'
'Why do we accept things the way they are?'
'It is the chosen word of the nonconformist, the defiant and the visionary.'
'If you're not afraid to ask "why?", you can change whatever you want.'

Television advertisements for Enron in the 1990s were brilliant and unsettling. Based on the tag line, 'Ask Why', they encouraged us to ask questions about the way we lived, and not to accept the status quo. At the time, it really seemed as if Enron could change everything, and that it was the company most likely to find the answers. It had grown in a little over a decade to be the seventh-largest company by revenues in the United States. At a time when the dot-com boom had generated hundreds of exciting companies with big ideas but hardly any revenues, and the great names of global commerce were hanging on to slowly growing revenues despite a widespread suspicion that they were clean out of creativity by comparison, Enron was the company that seemed to combine the two.

When Enron encouraged us to ask 'why?', it did so because it thought it had found the answers that no one else could find.

Jeff Skilling, the man who built Enron as its chief operating officer (COO), was the answer-finder in chief. By the turn of the millennium he had a track record: he had created the economic miracle that had made Enron what it was. But while Enron was ultimately killed by the need to keep creating growth, at the heart of its demise was the problem that Enron's answers weren't as good as it pretended they were.

As each set of businesses delivered fresh losses, Enron's creativity gradually turned in on itself. It became a business that wasn't so much dedicated to successful innovation as the appearance of successful innovation. Its accounts became more difficult to understand – not least because they were hiding around $30 billion of debt. Enron was intolerant of journalists and aggressive with analysts.

It encouraged us to ask 'why?', but when it declared profits year after year, it wasn't so keen for us to ask 'how?'.

Inspiration

Enron didn't exist until 1985, when it was formed by a merger of two smaller gas supply companies.[16] Even afterwards, under its chief executive Ken Lay, it was not a spectacular success. Supplying electricity and gas was difficult and bureaucratic. It had to build and operate 37,000 miles of pipelines and supply networks while dealing with complex regulation. In growing its business in the late 1980s, Enron took on massive amounts of debt: two years after the merger, Enron's debt was already 75 per cent of its market capitalization. Despite all the innovation, Enron never escaped from the problem that it was vulnerable to a falling share price.

Skilling's first coup for Enron came before he was even part of the company: as a consultant for McKinsey he advised Enron that it could set up a 'gas bank', to solve the problems of deregulation and fragmentation in the gas market, lending money to gas producers who would pay it back with guaranteed gas supply. Enron set up Gas Services in 1990, and Skilling joined the company.

The Gas Bank, though not wildly successful, showed Skilling's talent for thinking up wild solutions to old problems. Few Harvard MBAs would have wanted to join a sleepy gas supply company, but Skilling knew there was potential for a revolution. His creativity inspired a generation of ideas that stretched the possibilities of deregulation to the limit in the supply of gas, electricity, water, and more. Enron was Fortune's most innovative company for six years in a row.

It created a new market so that companies could hedge their investments against unpredictable weather: if there was a warm winter, gas suppliers need not take a hit.

It created a platform to sell network bandwidth, 'like a pork belly', as its advertising claimed, trading capacity that was then sold at a fixed price for 10 years at a variable price for days or hours.

From the outside, the innovations looked perfect: transforming everything they touched, creating efficiency, blowing away the competition, trading aggressively to capture market share.

From the inside, Enron had become a giant Ponzi scheme, whose future profits had been recognized today, and where creativity wasn't about doing profitable business – it was about doing any business you could do.

Living for the moment

The most important innovation of all, and the beginning of Enron's slide into oblivion, was the permission that Skilling received from the SEC to use mark-to-market accounting.[17] Enron was selling contracts to deliver gas or electricity for many years, with a short-term fixed price and a longer-term variable price. Enron argued that its 'volumetric product payments' had a predictable future cash flow, so they were assets. The value of the asset was found by estimating the price of the commodity over the life of the contract, and adding the whole thing together after discounting for inflation.

Mark-to-market meant that, as soon as a contract was signed, it could be recognized as revenue. The permission from the SEC was supposed to be temporary, but then it never called back. Enron, having used the technique in its 1991 report, wasn't going to remind the SEC.

Enron employees were delighted: it was, in effect, permission to write your own bonus. It was almost impossible to calculate the future prices, so employee estimates could easily be revised upwards if they needed to make a target. Some markets were dominated by Enron, and so the technique was known internally as 'mark-to-Enron'.

It also provided the perverse incentive that Enron could grab business by undercutting the market price. If the contract made a loss in years one to five, but a notional profit in years six to 10, it could be recognized as a profitable revenue. Enron was booking contracts to supply gas and electricity that it didn't have, and had to purchase at prices greater than it was selling for in the short term.

So many mark-to-market transactions were being done that the assessment and control group, which was supposed to be checking that the prices were appropriate, didn't have time to do the job. It was checking that the traders had got their sums right, but not whether the numbers bore any relationship to the outside world. Problem was, Enron had to keep writing contracts.

A bigger splash

Another problem with Enron's innovation was that it inevitably took the company out of markets it knew well, and into increasingly speculative gambles where its ideas didn't work.

The most obvious was bandwidth trading: an idea which the telecoms industry liked the sound of, but never had a hope of making any cash from. It was opportunistic: having inherited 1,500 miles of fibre optic cable from an acquisition, Enron Broadband Services (EBS) laid another 11,000 miles of cable in the next two years. But in its core markets, it dominated; it had stable prices with positive margins, and it didn't have established competition. In broadband, none of the above applied – not least because so much fibre had been laid that prices plunged. In 2000, EBS lost $60 million – despite a June deal in which it sold $100 million of unlit (unused) fibre optic cables to an off-balance-sheet subsidiary, which sold on most of the capacity to another Enron subsidiary at a notional price of $113 million in December. The deal suggested that prices between June and December had climbed by 53 per cent. In the open market, prices had fallen 67 per cent.

Similar problems beset the plan to trade water. 'First of all, you can't warehouse water. Second, water's not a commodity. It even has religious connotations. And it is very hard to transport, so you can't get a derivative contract or a buy-and-sell contract', points out Professor Malcolm Salter of Harvard Business School, who studied Enron's attitude to innovation.[18]

The adverts looked great, but Enron was expanding away from things it was good at, into things it didn't know how to do, and for which there was no business plan.

Where's the money?

Enron's income between 1996 and 2000 rose from $580 million to $970 million – at least on the balance sheet it did. Executive benefits were spectacular: in 2000, the top 200 employees shared $1.4 billion, more than seven times what they had earned two years earlier.

The increasing need to create a good story at the end of each quarter placed the responsibility on CFO Andy Fastow, in the opinion of *CFO Magazine* in 1999, 'the most creative financial officer of the year'. If only they had known how creative he really was.

Fastow's expertise was in securitization: packing up debt and selling it again. To clean up the balance sheet, he created Special Purpose Entities, or SPEs. The SPE would borrow from outside lenders. At the time, accounting rules specified that an independent owner needed to own 3 per cent of the SPE, and exert control. In reality, the 3 per cent was always a friendly partner, and the SPEs existed to soak up Enron debt, and keep it off the balance sheet in the short term.

LJM1, the first SPE, raised $15 million. LJM2 was much bigger: $200 million. At the end of Q3 in 1999, Enron sold seven assets to the SPEs, and bought five of them back after the next quarter had begun. From these transactions, Enron claimed revenues of $229 million.

A fall in the market

'The goal was basically to maintain the credit rating, which was actually a very low credit rating, but still investment grade', Prof. Salter explains. 'Any hiccup in terms of earnings or a cash flow decline would affect their rating.'

In February 2001, Skilling finally became CEO, but at exactly the wrong time. Broadband was costing a lot of money, with investments in Brazil, Argentina and the UK. The share price had begun to fall, as some investors couldn't work out what Enron did any more, and couldn't work out where the money was being made from reading the company literature. In March, *Fortune* published an article which questioned how Enron's stock price could be justified by its assets. The stock continued to plunge. By August, Skilling resigned for 'personal reasons'.

The stock continued to fall. Some employees were now questioning Enron. Andersen, Enron's accountant, decided that the accounting for SPEs had been a breach of regulations. The accounts had to be restated in October, with $1.2 billion less equity.

Still the stock was falling – worth about a quarter of what it had sold for only a year earlier. By 24 October, Fastow had been fired and the SEC was launching an investigation. On 2 December 2001, Enron was bankrupt. Employees were given 30 minutes to leave the building. Enron shares, which many of them had bought as part of a retirement plan, were worthless. Later they found that Enron senior executives, while reassuring them that the company was about to turn the corner, had cashed in $1 billion of their shares.

There's plenty of blame to go around at Enron: traders who behaved unethically, auditors who were prepared to stretch the truth and look the other way, senior staff who knew that there was no long-term future in what they were doing, but carried on.

Prof. Salter has looked at how the senior management operated. Everything was done in a hurry, without the necessary checks. Either they thought that Enron was running smoothly, or they knew it wasn't and didn't want to take the responsibility. 'The average meeting length of the audit committee and finance committee that I could glean from looking at the agenda was about 90 minutes', he says (normally they would last at least a day).

There was recklessness, and there were incentives to do the wrong thing, and a lack of ethics, but Prof. Salter points out that, if we hadn't adored Enron quite so much, the crash wouldn't have been quite so surprising or sudden. It might not have happened at all, because then the right questions would have been asked.

> There's a social part of this. *Fortune* and a variety of other magazines anointed Skilling, Lay and Fastow as rock stars. To a certain extent they became so powerful that the board became their adoring fans. So I think there was a real imbalance of power. The executive didn't work for the board.

The numbers game

'Capitalism needs accountants', writes the economist Joseph Stiglitz. 'If the firm could make up any old number, who would buy a share?'[19]

Anyone who has ever used the services of an accountant knows that the rules merely set boundaries. Inside those boundaries, there are principles. Inside those principles, there is wiggle room.

The wiggle room serves a useful purpose in an ideal world: it allows a company to present its figures in a way that reflects the work it is doing, while still ensuring that you can compare two balance sheets and understand the strengths and weaknesses of the companies that prepared them. It also allows the company to account for the same business in a tax-efficient way. That's our system.

The decisions start at the micro level. Stiglitz, in his book *The Roaring Nineties*, offers this example: A movable wall in a modern office building is furniture. So it depreciates (that is, the value declines in the accounts) over 10 years. This raises the company's cost of doing business, reduces profits, but means it pays less tax. Or it could be part of the building. In which case, its value depreciates over 30 years. That raises income, which investors like, and would boost the share price, but it will pay more tax.

So far, so good. The company uses an external firm of accountants, and works alongside it. The company adjusts its books to reflect its priorities in this way, and the external auditors for the accounting firm check whether those numbers reflect what is known as 'Generally Accepted Accounting Principles', or GAAP. Rules are not observed or broken, as much as principles are adhered to, stretched, and occasionally ignored.

The big accounting firms have two distinct functions: advisory, which tells the company the best way to account for its office walls; and audit, which checks that it is within GAAP. These are separate. There is, however, the potential of a conflict of interest when a client contract is worth many millions, and the client has ambitions that stretch the tolerance of GAAP.

Even within the rules, the complexity of modern accounting practice creates situations where a company gets the best of both worlds using an accounting sleight of hand. In the moving wall example, if the accountants created what is known as a 'special entity', the movable walls could be categorized as both furniture and building simultaneously. The client pays less tax but gets a higher share price too. Walls are not very important, but what happens off the balance sheet, as Enron showed, can often be more important than what we see on it.

A question of trust

'Reporting can be pretty complex, and that's down to the nature of the society that we live in. We expect it to be easy, but that's not the reality', says Dean Krehmeyer, a former accountant and consultant and now executive director of the Business Roundtable Institute for Corporate Ethics,[20] where CEOs of companies that want to demonstrate ethical accounting practices can work out exactly what those practices might be. That, he says, is not an easy problem to solve. 'Companies often don't have material misstatements. That doesn't mean we can trust what they have to say to the letter', he warns.

There are several problems. The first is that, not surprisingly, the most adept readers and creators of financial information are in the business of creating it. Our financial literacy is way behind theirs. They lead innovation, and we try to catch up. But with hundreds of reports and financial statements every day, even sophisticated readers have limited ability to drill into what the figures mean. That means it's hard to tell legitimate, but aggressive GAAP from deception.

The second is that we overstate the job of the auditor. 'Do accountants have responsibility to detect fraud? I would argue that almost all of us would say, "yes". That's not technically what accountants are engaged to do in an audit. We need to bridge that gap, and regulation has proved inefficient and incomplete', says Krehmeyer. An external auditor sees figures after they have been consolidated internally. An example: a manufacturer in China makes your products under licence. It underpays its licence revenues. It may be the job of an internal auditor to check them, but this might destroy a profitable relationship, so it will only do this if there is clear evidence of fraud. Having been signed off by the internal auditor, it is outside the scope of an external audit. But fraud it is.

This becomes even more complex thanks to outsourcing, globalization and mergers. It's no longer clear exactly which economic activity on the balance sheet that turns out to be fraudulent happens within a company, which happens outside with tacit approval, and which happens outside, but the company would stop if it knew.

The third is that the auditors are influenced by the need to win, and keep, business. That rarely means 'looking the other way', but it clearly influences what it will find to be acceptable GAAP in some cases.

Arthur Andersen

The auditor for both Enron and WorldCom – and Sunbeam, covered later in the book – was Arthur Andersen. It has become the focus for those who claim that the conflict of interest between the need to generate business, and the need to restrain CEOs who overreach, inevitably sometimes results in unethical practice.

Formerly one of the five giant accounting firms that divvy up the auditing jobs for successful companies worldwide, Arthur Andersen still exists, but as a tiny rump of a firm that once employed 85,000 talented people. It has more than 100 civil lawsuits outstanding against it, and the staff working for the firm are engaged in settling them.

Working closely with Enron initially brought prestige to the firm, but it is now chiefly remembered as the firm that shredded a ton of documents before investigators saw them. 'The evidence available to us suggests that Andersen did not fulfil its professional responsibilities in connection with its audits of Enron's financial statements', was the conclusion of the Powers Committee,[21] which investigated the collapse of Enron on behalf of the board.

The question of what Arthur Andersen was guilty of has not been resolved. The firm did help shred documents relating to its audit of Enron before investigators could see them, on the instructions of two of its managers. In June 2002, the company was convicted of obstruction of justice, and so was forced to surrender its licences to audit public companies.

In May 2005, the US Supreme Court overturned the conviction on the basis that the instructions to the jury were too vague, and could lead them to convict even without evidence. Arthur Andersen could resume its auditing work tomorrow, if anyone would employ it – or if it had anyone left to do the work.

Is Andersen's fall an example of the legal system, and the market, exercising appropriate discipline on its failures? If you consider that the firm had an ethical duty to exercise stronger control on those companies, then all that has happened is that one business failure became several. If it performed its duties adequately in this case, we might legitimately ask whether external auditors have a useful function.

For a corrupt or bullying CEO, the business can become primarily a way to deliver numbers – whatever the quality of the audit (though a lax audit might open some doors on occasions). Public companies are subject to the demands of the markets. Approval, expressed through the share price, doesn't just mean that the company has the equity to invest in growing its business, but also that the chief executive and the management team keep their jobs. So the CEO has both a professional and a personal incentive to look good, and the team that delivers the numbers are dedicated to making that happen.

That means looking good every three months. Quarterly reporting has become part of the soap opera story of big-name companies. If, as a public company, no one cares about your quarterlies, it's because you're not important enough to be a success.

'CEOs say "we don't have the chance to explain our numbers". Stakeholders pressurize us to compartmentalize our business into bite-size nuggets', says Krehmeyer, who is sympathetic to those managers who see themselves as victims of the problem of short-termism. 'All of us, as individuals, should take it as our responsibility to strengthen our curiosity. Not to look at earnings per share, but to understand where those earnings came from. Should we care so much what the earnings are in the next quarter, if the company has great long-term investments? CEOs are now in post for an average of slightly over three years. And the average time a share is held is less than a year. When the balance tips towards the short term at the expense of the long term, it creates perils.'

Business in peril

The perils are that the quarterly, and even annual, earnings are skewed to tell a good story. The most extreme example is when the company reports both GAAP and non-GAAP figures, while assuring its investors that the non-GAAP measure is a more accurate reflection of the state of the business. This sometimes blurs the boundary between reporting and storytelling, and its widespread use was pioneered by the dot-com firms, who often needed to tell a good story most of all. They (correctly, in some cases) pointed out that their early costs were the necessary price of building a global business, and so a GAAP balance sheet couldn't be compared to that of an oil company or supermarket.

Which is fine, as long as when you look at the GAAP figures and the non-GAAP figures side by side, you can see how one was adjusted to become the other. Try it on a selection of press releases, which often headline the non-GAAP measures, deliver the numbers, and then report the GAAP quarterly earnings. It's not always easy to see how they relate.

The popular non-GAAP measure of EBITDA – earnings before interest, taxes, depreciation and amortization – is an example, which successfully makes headlines. It is effectively the company's operational cash flow, and has become popular among technology and telecoms companies with a lot of interest to pay on debt, or expensive assets whose value declines rapidly. It adds a lot of good news together, and doesn't subtract a lot of bad news. On one hand, it helps to compare which companies are actually doing profitable business, day to day. On the other, it can lead to a misleadingly happy picture, because the cost of servicing that debt, or the banks' willingness to refinance, can change the picture rapidly.

Responsible companies show, in detail, how EBITDA reconciles with the GAAP measure of net earnings, which will often be negative while GAAP is positive.

The most important problem when you have to deliver numbers that show you are fit is that, if you don't deliver them, confidence collapses – and your business needs confidence, because your share price and ability to raise debt depend on that. The bosses of Enron, Madoff (not a public company, but one evaluated even more closely on its ability to generate positive returns on investment – because that's all it did) and WorldCom all made decisions that, if it weren't for the need to show consistently improving results, they wouldn't have made.

'Organizations become so focused on meeting next quarter's earnings-per-share targets that manipulation is going on specifically to meet the targets. This isn't always accounting manipulation. We're talking about real business decisions that are taken which destroy value. Many companies reduce R&D, decrease advertising spending, they don't hire essential staff. They might meet their 90-day target, but it's the wrong decision over two or three years', says Kreymeyer.

It doesn't help that many companies now have adopted the practice of giving detailed quarterly guidance – predicting revenues and profits for the next three months. They don't have to do it, but it has become a way to manipulate the consensus view of the near future, and influence the share price.

Problem is, when those three months are up, the markets punish companies that don't make their guidance at least as badly as they discount those that gave no guidance at all. If you're a CEO who can predict the future and make it come true, you're a hero. It's an extra incentive, in a few cases, for even successful companies to cheat. After all, if you always outperform, it's far more remarkable when you miss your target. You were a hero, now you're a zero – even if the numbers look terrific in the long run.

Making your numbers is positive. Having to make too many numbers every time, when you've successfully created the image that you are too good to fail, can have disastrous – and illegal – consequences.

Chapter Three
It worked last time

"These deals are a little bit like morphine. It's very hard to come off them. **ELIZABETH MONRAD, FORMER CFO, AIG**[22]

When you're in a fight, winning is much better than losing. And winning big is much better than winning small.

The nature of success means that the small bets made at the beginning get doubled and doubled, like an obsessive roulette player who keeps betting everything on black because that worked last time. It kills some companies slowly, some quickly. But if this is the strategy, it will kill you in the end.

There are more than 300 press releases a day in the English-speaking world which promise that something is innovative. Nothing is more alluring. It was the promise of ceaseless innovation that created a generation of dot-com chief executive officers (CEOs).

Yet success, for many companies, produces the effect that you follow the same path as you did before, just with higher stakes. Often this is painted as being innovative and revolutionary, but now there are powerful forces that prevent radical change.

The most powerful is that, when you become part of the company, or invest in it, you're following in the footsteps of people who did very well by doing a certain type of thing: they are either rich and powerful, or the senior management of the company. If you think it's wrong, your voice is drowned out.

The second is that companies, especially successful ones, have a variety of ways to communicate the rightness of their vision. Their marketing naturally concentrates on their success. Their public relations effort makes sure that newspapers write about it. Their internal communications pass on the company's values. Also, we simply absorb the values and culture. We come to believe that it's right because the company does it, rather than that the company did it in the past because it was the right thing to do.

An example is the tendency of fund managers to 'herd'. They are measured relative to each other. We invest in funds with the best return in their class. It provides a powerful incentive to follow the crowd if you are in charge of making the investments, because if you do exactly the same as your competitors, you won't do any worse than them – even if what you do is not optimal. If everyone is buying into bowling alleys, then bowling alley shares go up, you all look equally good, and no one notices in the short term that the share price of the lucky firms no longer represents the true value of the asset.

The failures in this section all took a success and pushed the idea to the limit because it had been successful. Until it wasn't.

Living above your means *Northern Rock*

We assume that successful companies are invulnerable. Yet by choosing to grow quickly, some expose themselves to fatal amounts of risk.

'Life changed on 9 August [2007], like snapping a finger', was how former Northern Rock chief executive Adam Applegarth described the beginning of the end of the bank that he built. 'Watching the liquidity disappear since then has been astonishing.'[23]

When there's a run on your bank, life changes quickly. He was giving his interview five weeks after the metaphorical finger-snap. In those five weeks, Northern Rock suffered the first run on a British bank in living memory, resulting in a £25 billion bailout from the Bank of England, nationalization, and redundancy for a third of its workforce.

Applegarth and his fellow directors became the first public symbols of the UK's credit crunch, and Northern Rock became a symbol for reckless excess. The strategy of the bank was branded 'reckless' by MPs in the Commons Treasury Committee.[24] But until the summer of 2007, Northern Rock had been one of the greatest success stories of regional development in the UK. It had been a bank that grew to be the fifth-largest in the UK without losing its roots in the community around Newcastle. It had generated huge profits, but ploughed 5 per cent back into the local community, rather than throwing it around in bonuses. It had created employment for 6,000 people in an area where high-quality jobs were hard to find, and had not outsourced those jobs offshore in a dash for profit.

When things were going well, Northern Rock was everything that capitalism in the community could possibly be. It's just that, at the heart of its business, Northern Rock was borrowing its way to disaster.

Bricks and mortar

The long housing boom of the early 21st century created many winners, and Northern Rock saw the opportunity to create even more. In January 1996, according to the Nationwide building society, the average house price in the UK was £72,483.[25] By January 2000, it was £98,772. In July 2007, the peak of the market, it had reached £189,316 – roughly 2.5 times what it had been 15 years earlier. If your house was worth £200,000 at the turn of the millennium – a modest house in London – you had earned more than the average household income between then and 2007 just by living in it.

It's not surprising that daytime television was full of shows encouraging you to buy a house and flip it for profit. In the commercial breaks, adverts encouraged homeowners to take the equity in their house and convert it to cash for cars or holidays. Getting 'on the ladder' was the thing to do. British consumers had financed economic growth with $1.3 trillion of debt, which magically got paid off as long as your house went up in value.

Home ownership, at over 70 per cent, was at its highest level in history in the middle of the 2000s. We had come to expect that a mortgage was a right, not a privilege.[26]

The only problem: if you didn't have any savings and earned the median wage of around £30,000, you hadn't got a chance. Traditional mortgage lending was capped at 3.5 times your salary – in this case, that would be £105,000. For many people, even a basic home was out of reach in these conditions. For banks whose growth depended on acquiring mortgage customers – of which Northern Rock was the purest example – new business would have to come from more creative lending.

The banks themselves didn't break any rules by encouraging this; but others did that for them.

Creative lending

When the BBC investigated the mortgage market in February 2004,[27] it found that it was being helped along by a new type of mortgage: the 'self-cert'. To get one of these, you simply went to a mortgage broker, who wrote down your salary on a form. The bank – Northern Rock was one of the banks that offered self-cert – guaranteed not to check. When the BBC's reporters went looking for a house, nine out of 10 mortgage advisers had a solution to the problem of a £30,000 income: lie about it, and you'll get a bigger mortgage.

The mortgage world had acquired what economists call a principal–agent problem.

The agent (a mortgage adviser who gets paid for each mortgage he or she arranges, in this case) is hired by a principal (a bank) to do its business. Both bank and mortgage adviser want to get the customer locked in. When all the information is shared, this is healthy – it's how more or less everything is sold. When not everyone knows everything there is to know about the creditworthiness of the customer, and when there is incentive for the agent to act in a way that benefits the agent but maybe hurts the principal, that's what's going to happen. When house prices are going up, it doesn't matter much: if the bank repossesses a house because the owner can't pay the mortgage, it ends up with an asset that's worth more than the loan.

Around this time I was introduced to a cleaner, who wanted to ask me about the best place for her and her boyfriend to buy a flat. She has worked out that, if she lived there for a year or two until she went back to her own country, and paid a mortgage during this time, it would be cheaper than paying rent. If she knew she was leaving, she didn't need to pay the mortgage for the last few months – they'd just walk out one day, she explained.

I pointed out that she couldn't get a mortgage. They both worked for cash. They didn't have an employer. Come to think of it, they didn't even have a visa.

That's no problem, she said, they already had a mortgage. The adviser who set it up had done one for lots of her friends. She couldn't believe that British banks didn't ask questions.

That's a principal–agent problem.

In 2004, the Council of Mortgage Lenders claimed that self-cert mortgages were 1 per cent of the total. The BBC consulted a mortgage broker, who claimed that 30 per cent of new mortgages were self-certs. The Financial Services Authority put the figure at 6 per cent.

But fraud wasn't the only innovation. 'Fast-track' mortgages also took the borrower's word without a compulsory check. The bank could validate applications, but if it did, and the story wasn't going to stand up to scrutiny, the mortgage broker would cancel the application and reapply.

Loans of 100 per cent, 120 per cent and even 125 per cent were available. The extra was an unsecured loan for legal and moving costs, which was wrapped into the mortgage payment. It was a competitive market, and the loans seemed rash to observers who were looking at the number of sub-prime bank repossessions in the United States. But in the UK, where prices were still rising, defaults were at about a third of what they had been in the last recession.

Gradually the acceptable multiple of salary increased. Banks were so keen to acquire customers that you didn't even have to lie to behave recklessly.

Low-start mortgages would fix a low rate for a year or two, then suddenly jump to unaffordable levels. Interest-only mortgages meant that you never repaid the value of the house, just maintained the size of the loan.

In 2006, the *Daily Mail* found that First National, part of GE Money, would offer customers with a good credit record and no other debts 7.5 times their income.[28] It meant that a couple earning £25,000 each could set up home with an interest-only £376,506 mortgage.

That meant two-thirds of the money they earned went on mortgage repayments every month. The lenders also required a savings scheme to help pay the principal. But payments would have to come out of the lucky couple's remaining disposable income, already less than £1,000 a month.

'Question is, what would that leave them to eat?' the feature concluded.

Low risk

The boom had been profitable business for Northern Rock. In July 2007 it announced that its pre tax profit for the first half of the year was £296.1 million. While in the United States there were already large numbers of borrowers defaulting on loans, this wasn't an immediate problem in the UK, where lenders expected that maybe house prices would stop growing so quickly, but wouldn't fall. In the UK there weren't enough houses – especially in the cities – and those that were being built were increasingly being snapped up by buy-to-let landlords.

In the first half of 2007, Northern Rock wrote more mortgages than any other UK bank – £10.7 billion of loans, about 19 per cent of all mortgages in the UK. It admitted that it would lose money by lending so aggressively, but that it would be worth it in the long term – because it was winning customers with a positive long-term value. It's lending was 'low-risk', it said.

It might have worked. Had it done so, Northern Rock would have achieved its goal to become the number three bank in the UK. Its social commitment to good causes in the North East would have been matched by the social usefulness of helping a generation of first-time buyers to own their own homes. Gradually, perhaps, it would have tightened procedures to weed out fraud.

Northern Rock wasn't directly undermined by principal–agent problems, or its own sub-prime customers. It collapsed inside a few weeks because it lent too much, too fast – and when its customers found out how much, they panicked.

By July 2007, Northern Rock had already issued one profits warning, a warning that at the time caused little concern. It was based on the obscure technicality that the London Interbank Offered Rate (LIBOR) rate had risen.

LIBOR was the rate at which banks in London lent money to each other for short periods of time, known as 'wholesale' lending. It's low most of the time, because banks trust that they will get their money back from other banks. Northern Rock was a big consumer of wholesale lending: it accounted for 75 per cent of the money it lent out as mortgages, and 100 per cent of the business plan.

The basic concept was financial genius. The bank borrowed at the LIBOR rate. It lent to householders at its mortgage rates, which were higher. It securitized the home loan debts, and sold them to other banks as ultra-safe financial products. Risky loans attracted higher rates of interest, and came with homes attached. The risk was priced. Defaults take a long time to build up, and so the bank could handle them as they arose. As long as the bank priced the risk appropriately, it could write a mortgage using another bank's money to everyone in the country, and Northern Rock was well on the way to doing that.

Until, that is, the finger-snapping happened in August 2007, when the European Central Bank injected €94 billion into the banking system to try to encourage banks to continue lending to each other. In the United States, the Federal Reserve does something similar. In the UK, the Bank of England declines to follow – and also says that it would not automatically step in to save a bank that was in trouble.

At that time, the only sudden change that could happen, happened.

Banks in the UK simply stopped lending to each other. As the first impacts of the credit crunch hit, banks suddenly stopped to consider: How big is their exposure? How big is our exposure if we lend to them? The banks knew they had no idea about the creditworthiness of each other's business, because they knew little about the quality of the loans the other banks had made, or who had bought those loans when they were packaged up and sold on. Each bank worried that it risked lending to a bank that wouldn't be around next month. House prices were diving in the United States, and the securitized mortgages (known in the business as collateralized debt obligations, or CDOs) created not just risk (you know what might go wrong, but you can select how much to charge to cover yourself if the worst happens), but uncertainty (if it hits the fan, your guess is as good as mine).

Risk, banks can handle, because buying risk at the right price is their job. If there is uncertainty, it's better not to buy anything, because you don't know how much to pay.

And so, with banks unwilling to lend, the LIBOR rate climbed until it stood at, or above, the mortgage rates that Northern Rock was offering. It couldn't get the wholesale loans it needed to finance its retail loans, because not enough liquidity was available at any price.

The last resort

On 14 August, Mervyn King, the governor of the Bank of England, who had previously sought to reassure the markets, was told by the Financial Services Authority (FSA) that there were liquidity problems at Northern Rock.[29] Within two days, Northern Rock chairman Matt Ridley called King to warn him that the Bank of England might need to step in temporarily. Northern Rock was suddenly looking for a buyer.

For several weeks, speculation mounted in the City about which banks were most exposed to the liquidity crisis, and Northern Rock couldn't begin to find a buyer. Banks didn't even want to lend money: they certainly didn't want to buy the company that maybe couldn't repay it. Finally, on the morning of 13 September 2007, the BBC revealed that the bank had been granted emergency support by the Bank of England, the UK's 'lender of last resort'.

The next day, according to Applegarth, it was 'business as usual'. Not so. The thousands of small investors who made up the other 25 per cent of the bank's deposits, many of whom had invested their life savings, had realized that UK law guaranteed only 90 per cent of the first £33,000 of their deposits. They wanted their money back, quickly. But Northern Rock's phones were jammed, and the website had collapsed under the load. As shares plunged 32 per cent, the streets outside the bank's 76 branches were packed with queues of customers who wanted to close accounts.

Luckily for 24-hour-news reporters, Northern Rock had been opening branches in the south of England, and so they could quickly be on the scene to interview worried pensioners, so that they could worry other pensioners too. Management complained that the bank was basically financially sound, which, thanks to the Bank of England's assistance, it was. But consumers had had their first whiff of the effect of the credit crunch. Finally the news media had an exciting way to explain the global financial crisis without having to run endless pictures of bank staff clustered round computer screens, and the length of the queue at Northern Rock was more grimly entertaining than the graph of the LIBOR rate.

Too late for Northern Rock, the Bank of England injected £10 billion into the money markets, and Northern Rock announced it was up for sale, after the Bank of England supported it with £25 billion. Ultimately, the government didn't think there was a viable offer for Northern Rock. Three years on, it owns the Rock, and hopes one day to sell it. Applegarth and his fellow directors, and their vision of a mortgage machine to hoover up every would-be homeowner, are gone too. The money machine that ran out of control lost £176.6 million in 2007, and £1.4 billion in 2008.

And yet the numbers of UK defaults have stayed relatively low. If the housing market had cooled, but wholesale lending had been available, Northern Rock might have survived, but with lower growth. It was killed not by its own risky loans, but the knock-on effect of loans that had been made by other banks, in another country.

The mortgage hysteria that drove Northern Rock's growth will not return in the near future. Our mortgages are not going to be a second salary any more. PricewaterhouseCoopers revealed in July 2010 that there is a 50 per cent chance that house prices, in real terms, will still be below 2007 levels in 2020.[30]

The 6.5 multiple of earnings and the 125 per cent loan are anecdotes we will tell our disbelieving children. Maybe we'll have plenty of opportunities because we will be living, like modern Walton families, in the spare room of our children's rented flats, because our pensions can't support us. It's not fair: we massaged the numbers on our mortgage applications for loans we could barely pay in 2007 because those houses would double our incomes. They were supposed to be our pensions.

After all, nobody, especially the bank, is supposed to lose money on a house.

Breaking the Queen's bank *Barings Bank*

When it appears that chasing a dream has paid off, there are two temptations: to believe you really are as brilliant as people say you are, and not to ask too many questions. Barings Bank made both mistakes, and so was ruined by its star employee.[31]

The losses which brought down Barings Bank in 1995, compared to the massive sums we are accustomed to hearing about in connection with Lehman Brothers or Bear Stearns a decade later, seem comparatively trivial. Barings Bank collapsed on 26 February 1995 when the Sultan of Brunei declined to organize a last-minute rescue. The losses generated by Barings' derivatives trading operation in Singapore were £843 million – less than 1 per cent of the bail out given to AIG. It is, however, one of the best examples of a dysfunctional merger that you could hope never to see. Barings was a merger between two businesses: one reflected the past, in which it was important, secure, conservative and reliable; the other represented the future, in which traders are aggressive, volatile and, if you don't watch them carefully, duplicitous.

Barings was, in the standard retelling, brought down by a 'rogue trader', Nick Leeson, who hid his aggressive trading strategy in a secret account, and piled losses on top of losses, while cooking the books to keep them out of sight of senior managers.

Leeson was, undoubtedly, the main villain. In the introduction to his autobiographical account of the collapse of Barings, he admits that it was 'a part of my life that I am trying desperately hard to leave behind'. Yet he strongly disputed the official version of events, contained in a Bank of England report on the collapse, in which other senior managers had little knowledge of what Leeson was doing until the bank collapsed around them.[32]

Even if we accept the Bank of England's report at face value, it doesn't alter what happened: an old-style institution, like a recently divorced middle-aged man, found a party-loving younger lover, and couldn't handle it.

The Duc de Richlieu said, in 1818,[33] that: 'There are six great powers in Europe: England, France, Prussia, Austria, Russia and Baring Brothers.' The bank, founded less than 60 years previously, had grown rich on speculative investment in new ventures, especially in North and South America. It soon joined the establishment. It lent money to France so that it could pay reparations at the end of the Napoleonic Wars. Even in the 1980s, when it had long since been surpassed by the great American investment banks, it still had the British Queen as a client.

In the 1980s, its rich tradition of investment was looking far from daring, and far from profitable. Barings was Old School. Its staff wore suits and ties and worked in wood-panelled offices. In the 'Greed is Good' years, the old banks began to look for new partners. Knowing that the industry was changing rapidly, Barings was one of many who looked for a merger with a stockbroking firm. It wanted Cazenove, almost as blue-blooded as Barings. It got Henderson Crosthwaite (Far East) instead.

One firm, two cultures

Barings and Henderson Crosthwaite had worked together in Far East markets, but at arm's length. Still, the consensus was that it was a good match: as close as Barings would find to a like-minded stockbroking arm, and – in truth – Barings in the Far East bore little resemblance to the stuffy British headquarters. The Far East business, catalysed by its stockbroking arm, was also operationally independent. So Barings Securities Limited (BSL), in the Far East, was entrepreneurial, trader-driven and informal; Barings Brothers & Co. in London was anything but. BSL hired a new generation of traders, who didn't have much education or good family ties, but did have a strong desire to make money.

One of those was Nick Leeson – but there were many more like him. BSL was 16 people in 1984, but 2,000 people by 1992. It was run by an aggressive manager called Christopher Heath, who was the most entrepreneurial of them all. He made the decisions, built the trading arm of Barings in his own image, and hired like crazy. So much so that one former manager, who left before the bank blew up, described the BSL management as 'second rate at best': 'They had no concept of the words risk and management going together, for instance.'

Leeson was well aware that the ordered, staid world of Barings in London didn't apply: when he arrived in Jakarta, he found that the Barings trading operation was being run from a room in the Hotel Borubudur. 'The reality of Barings was shoddy and inefficient', he wrote later.

Leeson had been hired for his back-office expertise. In operations like BSL, the back office does all the tedious paperwork, while the front office does the trades. The back office has to make sense of the business the traders are doing, account for it all, spot mistakes and try to rein in unauthorized or illegal behaviour. They are largely unsuccessful at this latter skill for two reasons. The first is that traders are smart, cunning, and often know how to either hide errors or at least disguise them a bit. The second is that traders are seen as the people who make the money, and who perform best when they are given freedom and a big bonus. Traders get the big money, the back office gets the long hours and, often, the blame when things go wrong.

In his book *Traders, Guns and Money*,[34] lifelong trader Satyajit Das points out how big a hole the traditional part of Barings was in, and how much it thought its traders (and one, in particular) were bailing it out. 'In the year Leeson's trading losses destroyed the bank, its total profits were about £37 million. Of this amount, Leeson's "profits" were £41 million... Barings had a system where 50 per cent of net profits were paid into a bonus pool... it was in no one's interest to stop the game.'

When he joined Barings, Leeson wanted to make the jump from the back office to the trading desk, and when he was transferred to Singapore in 1992, he passed his exams for a trader's licence. By 1993 he had been appointed assistant director and general manager of Barings Futures Singapore Pte (BFS), a new venture that was supposed to be using arbitrage to make risk-free trades in the Far East futures markets.

Internal rules forbade BFS from trading overnight with its own money: it had to settle up its own account every day. It could take overnight options (betting on the movement of markets) only on behalf of clients, not on its own account. This was the crazy new world of derivatives viewed through the traditional staid Barings lens. 'Arbs' are hard work and need a lot of capital for a small profit. In 1994, Leeson apparently made £30 million of profit for his employers from the tiny differences in prices that arbitrage creates. That's what the records show.

Borrowing from itself

Leeson, meanwhile, was exploiting the lack of supervision by running an unauthorized '88888' account, in which he was taking overnight positions which he was nominally prohibited from doing, and also trading between a known account and this secret account.

The account was created as a place to park errors, when the wrong trade is accidentally entered, for example. The 88888 account quickly became a place to hide unauthorized trades. Any losses for 88888 would be replenished by Leeson's increasingly volatile trades – he hoped. In the meantime, 88888 had to be kept afloat by borrowing money from other parts of the business. Leeson claimed it was a sort of bridge, while clients paid up for business he had done on their behalf.

It's a testament to the naïvety (at best) of the Barings management that they never questioned how dramatic profits could be made from arbitrage – taking a position in one market, and an equal and opposite position in another market, where the price was slightly different. It was their good fortune to have an apparently gifted performer like Leeson on board, and their even better fortune that no one else had spotted how these simple profits could be made.

Chairman Peter Barings, who 18 months later would be begging the governor of the Bank of England to lend his bank the money to survive, commented in September 1993 that 'it was not actually terribly difficult to make money in the securities business'.

Barings Bank had, effectively, outsourced the job of making money to one man. It had, also, left that man without supervision. The non-merger merger had left Barings with no clear lines of management. Traders reported to product managers, but also to the local manager. The back office reported to local managers and to the head office. Senior management managed by committee. BSL's massive trading business had an audit department of three.

Leeson reported to the chief operating officer (COO) of Barings Securities Singapore Limited, but also to the managing director, who thought that Leeson was reporting to London. London thought that the local COO was managing Leeson, but the local COO was upset that London was involved, so he took only a small interest in Leeson's unit. On the product side – the people who were responsible for profitability – there were at least four managers to whom Leeson was reporting, in two product groups.

Frequent reorganizations had created tensions between managers, who resented being interfered with, or having problem areas dumped on them, and some of the managers weren't even speaking. The old-school, committee-based approach from London had broken down.

Through this, Leeson kept trading, hiding ballooning losses in 88888. At the end of 1994, he was down £200 million. His bosses accepted the barely believable story that the £200 million was simply owed by clients, when the hole was sitting in 88888.

Worse: on 17 January 1995, Japan suffered the Kobe earthquake. Leeson's open positions suffered. He compounded the losses by betting that the Japanese stock market would recover. At the beginning of 1995, he was losing £11 million per day for his employers. Every day he would try to gamble more to get back to zero. The positions he was taking were now huge.

To do this, Leeson had to ask for larger and larger amounts of credit from head office. By the time Barings collapsed, he had cumulative funding of £740 million, twice the capital that Barings possessed.

Who's in charge?

'I was astonished that nobody stopped me', he wrote in his autobiography, recalling that only a few weeks before Barings collapsed, he had been in conversation with his chairman in the Singapore office. Leeson half expected to be arrested, but the chairman casually asked him about the market, and invited him to dinner. He claims that his many managers 'should have known that the daily requests for cash were totally wrong'. If one of the managers 'had really thought about what I was doing, he'd have seen that it was impossible'.

During January, the market rumours were that Barings had taken huge positions (it had) and that it was out of its depth (it was), and that when it had to settle these accounts, it would not have enough capital to do so (it didn't).

Compounding their failure to manage Leeson, when the rumours reached London, management did not investigate. Leeson was a star trader; without him they'd probably be out of a job. The trading operation was single-handedly making up for losses in the rest of the bank. Managers claimed they assumed that the rumours were based on the markets seeing one side of an arbitrage (for example, buying at 100 in one location), while not spotting that it was selling the same product at 105 in another market at the same time. In reality, it was Barings management that was seeing only half the picture.

Sublime incompetents

While there is no evidence that Leeson's superiors knew what he was doing – and the mess of reporting and management that Barings had created at the very least establishes that it was nobody's sole responsibility to find out what he was up to – the fact that two members of Barings management did not fly to Singapore before February to try to establish whether there was something wrong was incompetent, at best. It didn't take them long to find the awful truth.

On 23 February 1995, Leeson flew off on holiday to Kuala Lumpur after a frantic day of trading, having tried to close his positions and make up his losses. 'I knew I'd lost millions of pounds but I was too frightened to find out,' he wrote, 'the numbers scared me to death.' He resigned, by fax, was later arrested in Germany, and was sentenced to six and a half years in prison in Singapore.

Leeson's 'Rogue Trader' reputation was guaranteed by the report that the Bank of England published only four months after the collapse,[35] which criticized senior management, but found no evidence that they knew, or suspected, what Leeson was doing. The Singapore government took a different view, and the Minister of Finance's report indicated a belief that senior management colluded with Leeson. Those senior managers dispute this conclusion.

At the least, a simplistic fraud, which required the involvement of local traders and back-office staff to cover, was allowed to grow for almost three years. It is clear that Barings senior management bought and encouraged a money machine which they did not begin to understand. As long as it kept making profits that the rump of Barings could not hope to emulate, the old school had little incentive to look harder. But had they looked closely, even one month before the truth came out, they would have discovered the truth. It would have been unpalatable, but the money machine would not have blown up one of the former six great powers of Europe.

This was exactly the conclusion of the Singaporean Minister of Finance's report, if not the Bank of England's: that the only way the management of Barings would not have known is if 'they had persistently shut themselves from the truth'.

The *Daily Telegraph*, which might have been expected to defend the Establishment management of the bank, editorialized when the Bank of England report was published: 'It defies the comprehension of an outsider that a single individual could have wreaked havoc for almost three years without detection.'[36] It called Barings' management 'sublime incompetents, blithely counting their own booty'.

At least some of those managers bought into something they didn't understand. But the fabulous profits from the derivatives operation presented outsiders with the illusion of success – an illusion manipulated by a resourceful, if not especially plausible, employee.[37]

Easy money *The Mississippi Company*

If financial engineering was a medicine, it would never get to market: it kills too many of the patients, because those who administer it never know when to say stop.

The belief that the best way to make more money is to take more risk has a long and ignoble history. Barings is a recent example, but we have been using financial engineering to get ourselves into trouble since financial engineering was invented. Mix engineering with populism, and you have a serious problem. But we knew this 300 years ago.

The Mississippi Scheme of 1719 and 1720 was one of the first opportunities for a nation to create a better future for its citizens based on financial speculation. Instead it ruined thousands of people and almost caused the collapse of a country. Which was unfortunate: because, if the man who created it had stuck to the principles by which he created it, he might have been a national hero in France, even today. And even if he was a Brit.

The Mississippi Company, like the English South Seas Company, was set up to make profit from the New World, generally believed to be the source of fabulous riches. France was facing a similar problem to that faced by most countries in the developed world today: the French government was running a national debt of 1.5 billion livres, with no immediately apparent way to get rid of it. According to the 18th-century Cambio Mercatorio,[38] and using the price of gold in the 18th century as a convertor, 1 livre is roughly equivalent to £10 today.

France was the most populous country in Europe, but that population was around 20 million.

The Duke of Orleans was running the country because Louis XV was still an infant. The Duke had a taste for financial engineering: according to the American writer Washington Irving, 'He had already tampered with the coinage, calling in the coin of the nation, restamping it, and issuing it at a nominal increase of one-fifth; thus defrauding the nation out of twenty per cent of its capital.'[39]

Irving, with the benefit of hindsight (he was writing 100 years later), derived an obvious conclusion that no one else involved at the time did: 'He was not likely, therefore, to be scrupulous about any means likely to relieve him from financial difficulties.'

I am the Law

Enter a Scottish adventurer called John Law, who bought the Mississippi Company – which had been established in 1684 to establish trade from the French-owned parts of America – at that time, much of the South – but was doing little business.[40]

Law, who had tried several financial engineering schemes in Scotland, as well as spending a large amount of time in casinos, had a bright idea to revive the Company, and to make money for the government while he did it. Simply put: he was going to privatize it. Law issued shares in the Mississippi Company which cost 500 livres each.

Initially no one cared very much about this wonderful scheme, and in 1719 prices for shares in the scheme even slipped to 300 livres. It was then that Law's genius for what we now call public relations kicked in.

He promised that he would buy shares in the company for 500 livres in six months, because of all the wonderful trade that the company would do. If you bought your share today, you would make a 60 per cent return at least. There was no risk, the public reasoned, and Law was connected to some of France's most powerful people.

Despite the fact that, behind the bravado, the Mississippi Company wasn't doing any business whatever, the public quickly decided that this man – as a personal friend and business partner of the French royal family – must know something. Share sales took off. Law offered to take on the French government debt and pay it off, in return for monopolies over the trade in tobacco and other commodities acquired through the company.

Today, banks buy bonds issued by companies that need to borrow money. The money they pay allows those countries to repay other debts, some of which are to other banks. Having been repaid, they can then invest in more government bonds. Law understood the importance of liquidity for the scheme. By repaying government debt, Law enabled the government to pay its creditors – many of whom were France's richest families. They could invest in turn in this scheme that everyone was gossiping about – which pushed up the price of shares in the company, and convinced more people that the Mississippi Scheme was credible.

Potentially, things could have stopped there. The shares might have stabilized, or even declined a bit. Trade links with America would have taken months, even years, to start to pay off – as they later would, after the Company was out of the picture – and France would have been saved in an orderly fashion. The evidence that we have indicates that was Law's idea. He was a little bit crazy – taking on the national debt of the nearest superpower is evidence of that – but he wasn't stupid.

The Duke, though, probably was both. He wanted the country to get very rich, very quickly.

The Mississippi Lords

When the French government started issuing money and lending it at small rates of interest, and allowing the Mississippi Company to sell its shares by offering credit, the shares were suddenly affordable for the working classes. A national frenzy resulted, and prices climbed by the hour. The frenzy centred around a house in Rue Quincampoix, which opened at seven o'clock every morning, to the sound of drums and bells. Law had split the stock into smaller units so that as many people as possible could afford to invest. The ruling classes of France proved to be great enthusiasts: the Duke de Bourbon, the Prince of Conti, the Dukes de la Force and D'Antin were nicknamed the Mississippi Lords because they were such enthusiastic stock traders. The social mobility was intoxicating, as poor and rich traded on equal terms. The government didn't mind: they were making, literally, a mint.

The church fell into line too: it told investors that God was okay with the Mississippi Scheme. The church's objection to usury didn't, it announced, extend to dealing in shares. Half a million people travelled to Paris specifically to invest. Or, considering that there was no produce from the New World, it's better to say they travelled to speculate.

We have the ingredients of a national fit-to-bustness: a grand scheme that is supported, and often encouraged, by the government; a regulatory environment that is not so much laissez-faire as almost compelling people to get in there and fill their boots; the active involvement of the ruling class and the church, who would previously have been expected to be aloof, or even hostile, to speculation. Add the evidence that ordinary people could make a fortune through buying shares that they couldn't hope to realize in their lives through work. As long as most people are poor, any speculation that offers them an opportunity to be less poor is going to be popular.

For people who had little or nothing to lose, the risk–reward equation was so unbalanced that there seemed no point in not being part of the action if you had the opportunity. You didn't have to be a long-term investor – a few hours turned out to be enough. Charles Mackay, in his *Extraordinary Popular Delusions*, tells of how one servant was sent to sell stock at 8,000 livres, but by the time he got to the stock-jobber, found out the price was 10,000 livres instead. He gave the 8,000 livres to his master, pocketed the difference, and left the country with a small fortune in his pocket.

Law was, for a time, the hero. Like many of the short-term heroes in this book, he relished the acclaim, and made himself available for admiring visitors. He didn't resent that common people were pocketing the profits, because he was common.

The best example of this was Law's own coachman, as Irving relates: 'Mr. Law's domestics were said to become in like manner suddenly enriched by the crumbs that fell from his table. His coachman, having made his fortune, retired from his service. Mr. Law requested him to procure a coachman in his place. He appeared the next day with two, whom he pronounced equally good, and told Mr. Law: "Take which of them you choose, and I will take the other!"'

Everyone was a winner. Local business did well, because every successful speculator had disposable income. Noblemen rebuilt their grand houses. 'It was remarked at this time,' Mackay says, 'that Paris had never before been so full of objects of elegance and luxury. Statues, pictures and tapestries were imported in great quantities from foreign countries, and found a ready market.' The few who chose not to invest were shouted down when they complained that most would be ruined. Didn't they see that everything had changed?

Show us the money

The stock hit 15,000 livres in the summer of 1720, which gave the company a nominal market capitalization of 7.5 billion livres. Law was the greatest business phenomenon of the times: he had saved the finances of France, rebuilt the country, and raised some ordinary people out of poverty. However, he had also quickly abandoned all his warnings that too much speculation would be risky. Maybe the government twisted his arm. Maybe he was enjoying himself too much.

When some of the noblemen who were the biggest investors decided that perhaps a company with no visible business might not be worth £75 billion, and sought to convert some of their paper back to gold and silver, the company was – unsurprisingly – unable to pay. The French government, which had issued more and more stock, against Law's advice, did its best to sustain the bubble. It even passed laws on the maximum amount of gold any citizen could own to stop everyone trying to cash in their paper. But the bubble burst. The shares declined in value as fast as they had risen. The investors left holding paper shares were ruined, and Law was chased out of the country, probably into Europe.

The French economy went south with him. It took years to rebuild the damage.

Once the saviour of ordinary working people, Law became a scapegoat for the French ruling classes who had not only agreed with his scheme, but had agitated for it, profited from it, and even gone to the market to trade in person. Law, conveniently absent when the blame was shared out, was public enemy number one of the ruined working classes, and became the subject of famous bawdy songs. 'One of them in particular counselled the application of all his notes to the most ignoble use to which paper can be applied', Mackay wrote.

Glory chasers *Leeds United plc*

The story of Leeds United plc is, says the man who knows, 'The Template of how not to chase glory'. That's not quite true: the first half of the story is a story of how a visionary group of managers and investors built a very good sports team. But sport is the ultimate example of how 'very good' is not good enough. In searching for the extra couple of per cent, Leeds United destroyed everything that it had created.

For a business where the ruthless pursuit of success on the sports field is a prerequisite, failure off the field has been a surprisingly frequent visitor to most football clubs, but none as spectacularly as Leeds. Since 1992, 53 English football clubs have been insolvent at some time – some more than once. In this respect, Leeds United is top of a very competitive league.

That glory-chaser-in chief, and the popular villain of the Leeds United crash, is Peter Ridsdale.[41] Ridsdale, a lifelong fan, was chairman of Leeds from 1997 to 2003, and though rise-and-fall stories are common (increasingly so) in sport in general – and football in particular – arguably no club has soared as high and fallen as fast as Leeds did. In seven years Leeds went from the verge of a European Champions League final to administrative receivership in the third division of English Football. Perhaps it's a comment on the crazy enthusiasm that continues to blight sports administration that this third level is, by a series of rebrandings, now known as 'League One'.

Our story begins in 1999. Leeds, a once-great club with a large and loyal following, was bubbling under the top tier of English football. With new manager David O'Leary in place, the board, with its four main shareholders (Jupiter Asset Management, Schroders, USB Warburg and BSkyB) decided to take a calculated risk: instead of attempting organic growth and a mid-table position every season, it would spend more money on players and facilities in a bid to grab glory, and the rewards that go with it. As Ridsdale recalls in his book on the subject, *United We Fall* (Pan, 2008):

> David persuaded the board that we'd challenge the very best if we invested more in top-quality players. A collective attitude of 'it's now or never' dawned on us all. Maybe I was scared of the backlash from the fans, and the *Yorkshire Evening Post*, who'd been clamouring for us to invest in the future. Maybe the fan within me overruled the chairman.

When we talk about 'calculated risks', it's worth looking at the calculations that those risks involve. Soccer clubs deal in big numbers and not so big ones. When Ridsdale took over Leeds United, its annual turnover was less than £30 million; even when he left, it was £80 million. A big number for 11 boys kicking a ball in public, but no larger than a small chain of shops. On the other hand, Leeds United is a large part of the life of hundreds of thousands whose feelings of self-worth correlate with the success of the club.

Feed the need

Nick Hornby captured the feelings of all sports obsessives in *Fever Pitch*:[42] 'I have measured out my life in Arsenal Fixtures, and any event of any significance has a footballing shadow. When did my first real love affair end? The day after a disappointing 2-2 draw at home to Coventry.'

To feed the neediness of fans, clubs need to purchase assets in the form of players. At the time he was in charge of the kitty, players cost £5 million, plus the same in wages, for the sort of staff O'Leary needed.[43] Their asset value varied wildly: a good player in the middle of a contract who is injury-free and playing well is worth more than you paid for him in most cases; but once you have less than 12 months left on your contract, your transfer value declines steeply. Once you are out of contract you can leave for no fee. Also, the type of assets a football club has suffer from injury and lack of form (or lack of form caused by a long-term injury). Some will get arrested.

In short, the only players that are worth what you paid for them are the ones you don't want to sell. Leeds, however, was very careful to track this. Each month Ridsdale prepared reports on the value of his assets, and the likely value in the future. He was trying to be careful. His big signings were financed using an innovative sale-and-leaseback scheme, which deferred the payments.

On top of this, sport is a brutal financial meritocracy. At the time, the prize money went up by £500,000 for every place above the bottom that you finished in the Premier League table; if you finished in the bottom three and were relegated, your television income would drop from around £25 million to £1 million in the next season; and if you finished in the top two (now top four) positions and qualified for the European Champions League, the revenue from a good run could be £20 million in one season. The play-off game that, every season, lifts one team into the top tier of the English football system is considered to be the most valuable football game in the world.

Add those together, without even thinking about gate receipts or Chinese TV deals, and as a rule of thumb the reward for success at Leeds could easily treble turnover compared to mid-table mediocrity.

But success, even for a fan of the club like Ridsdale, was a two-way street. In 1999, an anonymous source quoted in *Business Age* summed up the binary nature of Ridsdale's job: he was involved in 'A dash for glory... if he pulls it off, he will be a hero. If he gets it wrong, the knives will be out.'

You can guess where this one's going. The speed and the ruthlessness of the descent, though, surprised everyone involved, not least Ridsdale. The route Leeds took shows the problem of combining two jobs: a lifelong fan and a boss. In the winter of 1999–2000 the young, optimistic club with its young, optimistic manager and its relatively young, popular chairman was on the top of the Premier League. Ridsdale was making the most of it. He was always handy with a quote for the newspapers, and was known to journalists as 'Publicity Pete'.[44]

Sporting clubs often find it hard to remain stable, because pure sporting performance needs unity of purpose on the pitch. When everyone believes the same thing, then there's the danger that no one is exerting financial restraint off it, because the business is infected with the same unity of purpose, and has the same self-belief. At Leeds, Ridsdale had made the error of extending this unity of purpose from the changing room to the boardroom. 'The problem that we didn't appreciate was that we didn't think the good times would stop. Failure was a taboo thought at a club drilled with a winning attitude', he recalls. At Leeds 'no one gave due care and attention to the road ahead. We just kept thundering on.'

It's hard not to do this when 40,000 fans sing 'There's only one Peter Ridsdale', and when your club reached the semi-final of Europe's largest football competition the next year. It has to be a factor when you approve the signing of Rio Ferdinand, at that time 21 years old, for £18 million, and a total outlay in two years of £64 million on players. The club sustained its wild ride, despite the problem that two of its best players were in court, accused of beating up a student outside a nightclub. On 1 January 2002, Leeds was back to the top of the premiership.

A car crash

'You don't sit there and say, "Hang on a minute, what happens if this all falls apart?"... our strategy was based on the drive for success, not the fear of failure', Ridsdale recalls. The trouble is that the hidden risks – players playing badly, arguments over tactics, other teams playing well, problems with the middle management – don't surface in years, but in days. For two months afterwards Leeds did not win a match. 'The ensuing four months was like witnessing a car crash as a helpless spectator', Ridsdale says. The club's spending on players touched £100 million, but the assets were declining in value as quickly as Leeds were going down the league table.

The sale-and-leaseback arrangements would have been wonderful if the club had the cash flow to make the payments, and had accumulated savings to make the final payments. Even if not, if the players were worth more than Leeds had paid for them, one or two could be sold, or the club could refinance. But Leeds was out of its depth, because no amount of financial engineering can make the players perform.

By the end of the season the club had not qualified for competition in Europe the next season. There wasn't fear of failure, because failure was suddenly real. The club made a £28.2 million operating loss in 2002 – £23 million worse than the previous year – and needed to find savings of between £30 and £40 million, immediately.

Football, again, is different: trimming budgets by about half your turnover is tough for any company, but if (for example) your Singapore office or your range of celebrity-branded perfume isn't working, a non-core business is a target for cost-cutting. Leeds did one thing that raised revenue: it played football once or twice a week for nine months every year. Everything else – the shirt sales, the sponsorship revenue – flowed from that.

There was very little it could cut that wouldn't make it much worse at doing its only job. A fire-sale of players managed to stave off administration, for a time, but it also signalled an end to the dream, the management career of O'Leary (at least, for now), and the job of Peter Ridsdale. Leeds tumbled down the leagues, and, though their fans have not deserted the team, the club has been in and out of administrative receivership to escape debts to all its 'non-football' creditors (such as the St John Ambulance).

Worth nowt

It's always emotional when a business fails, doubly so when that business is a part of your self-image in some way.

In 2003, fans hung a sign outside the ground: 'January Sale – 1 set of loyal fans (worth nowt to a plc)'. Ridsdale's successor accused him of extravagance, pointing out that he was paying £20 a month for a fish tank. In the odd world of football finance, the accusation of keeping fancy fish continues to haunt Ridsdale. On the other hand, the yearly fish bill would not have paid the wage bill for one of his assets to put on his kit.

Ridsdale warns that we 'should perhaps look at the story of Leeds United and realize that the finances, fortunes and gambles inherent within this volatile market don't make the "mighty whites" a unique and pitiable exception'.

True; but it's not the finances and fortunes that condemn football's dreamers so often. It's the dream itself. In Ridsdale's time, only two clubs in the Premier League could progress to the European Champions League, where they would meet equivalent clubs from all over Europe – also hoping for the opportunity to make the progress that would generate the money they had already spent. It wasn't that the rewards weren't there, but that the chances of realizing them, even if nothing unusual occurred, were tiny. Ridsdale got the job in part because he loved Leeds United. Ultimately, it made him blind to the true picture of failure. After he resigned he told Phil Rostron, then the sports editor of the *Yorkshire Evening Post*, that 'they just criticize you for it and say, "you shouldn't have taken the risk", but at the time we didn't think it was a risk. Otherwise, we wouldn't have done it.'

Former deputy chairman Allan Leighton, whose experience as chairman of the Royal Mail gives him an insight into a business that can't dare to dream, was alongside Ridsdale during the good times and the bad. What, we should ask, blinds one of the UK's most hard-headed businessmen to the realities of football finance? 'There are lessons to be learnt for teams the world over from what happened in Yorkshire', he said in 2005, after he had stepped down. Perhaps lesson one is that, if you recruit fans to run your business, you can't rely on them for rational risk management.

For the experienced football writer Paul Hayward, the rationalization that Leeds were just chasing success isn't good enough. 'The most insidious deceit to invade English football's phrase book in this age of boom and bust is still Leeds United's post-implosion claim to have been "living the dream". They were not. They were living the lie... It was a feature of Britain's suicidal recklessness in banking, the housing market and football that problem gambling was recast as entrepreneurship', he wrote, as Portsmouth FC outdid Leeds by becoming the first English league club to slip into administrative receivership while it was still in the Premier League, having passed through a succession of owners. If other football clubs have learnt anything positive from Leeds, it's not obvious yet what that is.[45]

Upselling the dream

Just as history is not made by great men alone, so companies and countries don't go bust because one or two people chase the dream too hard. They need a support staff.

If you're a modern CEO, there are hundreds of people dedicated to convincing thousands of other people that your dream is the best dream that it's possible to have. It's their job, and they're very good at it; but their role isn't so different from the Mississippi Lords. They create enthusiasm.

Two old acquaintances once described how difficult it was to explain to their mothers what they did:

One: I can't tell my mother that I work in public relations, so I tell her I work in marketing.

Other: I just tell mine that I work in London.

The process of forming and influencing opinion is subtle, important, lucrative, and hard to understand if you're outside it. The modern corporation has internal marketing and marketing communications, who tell people about the internal marketing. It will have external agencies. Advertising is the most obvious, and marketing, to help the internal marketing people and give the internal marketing communications people something else to communicate. The public relations companies (there will be more than one) specialize in different aspects of opinion-forming. Some concentrate on financial relations: they deal with the City pages of newspapers. Some deal with consumer perception, some with how the business looks to outsiders. One or other of them will deal with financial and industry analysts, and there will be someone with the thankless task of keeping bloggers excited.

The internal and external communicators will help TV companies by giving them ready-made pictures of the company headquarters on a sunny day, and happy people using the products. There are shots of the inside of super-clean factories, and even re-recorded interviews with the CEO making bland comments.

It gets more exotic. Some employ agencies to read online forums, intercept and comment on criticism. There's even a new generation of 'word of mouth' agencies, which can do something as ordinary as putting up a fan page on Facebook for the company, or it can pay people to 'big you up' in pubs and shops.[46]

And then, of course, there are the lobbyists, who don't just pitch for the company to Members of Parliament; they bat for the entire industry, to create legislation that's friendly to their aims.

All of which is designed to create a culture in which we think well of the companies that are sending out the message. They don't lie – well, not often – but they omit, and frame. That's the job. It's not a crime, unless we choose to ignore what's left out.

But it's hard to know what's been left out because, by definition, we don't see it. It's de-emphasized. Journalists who upset companies are frozen out and denied access. There's an informal patronage system, in which friendly journalists are fed stories 'off the record', or given interviews with senior executives. This suits both sides: the journalist gets a cover story; the CEO knows that the interviewer is likely not to be too testing, and copy will most likely be friendly.

This isn't a job for idealists, but it's not purely cynical. Many people inside and outside the company who work in communications believe the dream too. After all, the first stage of selling it is to sell it to your own staff. If the management can't do that, it's a waste of time taking it out to other people. And, let's not forget, it's their job.

Lie to us again

The emphasis on framing a positive message for your company or your industry creates momentum. And momentum can be just as strong behind bad ideas as behind good ones.

How easy is it to manipulate the media? The meeting of G20 leaders in London on 1 April 2009 is a useful case study of how surprisingly easy it might be. The key is to catch the momentum at the right time, and know that a fresh story is always going to catch our attention.

Planting a good-news story helps us to feel optimistic about our futures. Banks that offered 110 per cent mortgages presented the story as a wonderful opportunity for young people to buy their first home. Companies disguise holes in their balance sheets by focusing on positive figures, no matter how obscure or unimportant they are. It's the job of the press to investigate, but a combination of ignorance and underfunding has strengthened the role of those who create the artifice of fitness when the company is closer to bustness.

Public relations, skilfully handled, can even make a bailed-out bonus-earning bank trader seem like a victim. You may recall the G20 demonstrations: the windows of an RBS bank were smashed. Demonstrators were surrounded by police, and 'kettled' – kept in one area to avoid running battles. The event had saturation media coverage and aggressive policing. We expected a riot. But why?

In the lead-up to the G20 summit, global public opinion was very much against the bailed-out banks. On 18 March 2009, the news looked bleak for banks: UK prime minister Gordon Brown called for tougher curbs on bosses' pay. The UK Financial Services Authority was recommending a global crackdown on bank excess. *The Observer* newspaper criticized the culture of big bank bonuses. It told us to 'Look no further than inequality for the source of all our ills.'[47]

The next day there was a new story. An unnamed senior police officer had, in conversation, warned of the potential of 'a summer of rage' in London, although the press office of the Metropolitan Police, when asked, was 'not aware of any specific threat'.

No matter. This, if your job is to rehabilitate the image of your banking staff, is a gift.

Three days later the unspecific threat had been crafted into a specific form. The London Chamber of Commerce was warning of riots[48] (though, at this time, the police were not). 'Businesses might want to consider asking their staff not to dress in a suit and tie' was the advice. By 27 March the press, having called a few small-time anarchists that they found on the internet and asked them to boast of what they wanted to do, had created an entirely new story: 'Bankers have been told to ditch their suits next week to avoid a beating from mobs of rioters', revealed the *Daily Star*, having been briefed by the press offices of the banks in question that yes, they were scared. 'Leave the flash car at home, spend the night in a hotel, hire a bodyguard. This is the kind of advice security experts are giving', said Reuters, having been told this by the security experts who were paid by the banks to give this advice.

By the date of the G20 summit, banking reform was off the front page of the popular press. Banks had become the victims of a more dangerous (though fictitious) mob. Vague stories of plans to block the Blackwall Tunnel or drive a stolen tank into the City were far more exciting than risk analysis and bonus caps. Reporters hung around on the edges of a crowd, looking for scuffles, flanked by amused demonstrators in fancy dress. There was some dangerous juggling and unicycling. A few spectators, penned in behind a line of police and two lines of photographers, obligingly scuffled, and a giant peace camp dedicated to exploring the possibilities of global reform of the financial system so that we wouldn't have to bail out the reckless risk-taking of banks again was completely ignored, even though it was about 200 yards from the news-gatherers who were waiting for the war to start.

The satirical newspaper *The Onion* summed up the change in mood a month later: 'Nation Ready To Be Lied To About Economy Again'[49] was the headline. 'After nearly four months of frank, honest and open dialog about the failing economy, a weary US populace announced this week that it is once again ready to be lied to about the state of the financial system.'

Peddling influence

Lobbying is a huge business, and a successful one for companies that do it well. Some lobbyists do the job for money, some do it because they're committed to the company they lobby for. They are just doing their job, which might mean propping up a failing car company by creating tariffs on foreign cars, or influencing regulatory approval for a merger that distorts the market, or amending legislation to make risky trading legal.

Lobbying is powerful because it creates an environment in which the company doesn't just get some favourable publicity. It gets a whole new market, or market structure. Or it stops legislation that would rein it in.

Whatever happens, powerful companies know how important lobbying is. That's why lobbyists, especially in the United States, are more powerful than they have ever been. 'The constitutional right enjoyed by every citizen to "petition government for a redress of grievances" has become a career option, an industry that is making some people very wealthy. Lobbying has become a $3 billion-a-year industry. It has doubled in size over the last six years', writes Lee Hamilton, director of the Center on Congress at Indiana University,[50] and a member of the US House of Representatives for 34 years. He says that lobbying is 'so intertwined with public life that it's impossible to tell if legislation is a legitimate "redress of grievances" or something less savory… it makes the entire legislative process suspect. Did this bill pass because it's best for the country, or because those with money had extraordinary opportunities to influence legislators that the rest of us lacked?'

The behind-the-scenes influence of the powerful was nowhere more apparent than in the workings of Enron, whose lobbyists contributed as much to the company as any trader or salesperson. Chairman Ken Lay was a handy fund-raiser for George Bush during the 1990s, and stayed over at the White House. Enron and its employees were the biggest corporate donors to George W Bush until 2001. Senior Enron executives contributed a total of $1.7 million to politicians in the 2000 election campaign.

'In their lobbying, they acted like the 800-pound gorilla they were', said Christopher Horner, a Washington lawyer who directed Enron's government relations in 1997. Its methods were, however, more sophisticated. For example, Enron set up 'Americans for Affordable Electricity', run by New York politician Bill Paxon. Its role was to recruit business support for deregulation.

A source of risk

Does this matter? It does, in two ways. The first is when companies under threat mount a public relations offensive using 'independent' experts.

Bernard Whitman is president of Whitman Insight Strategies, a communications firm that specializes in helping 'guide successful lobbying, communications and information campaigns through targeted research'. Whitman's clients have included lobbying firms like BGR Group and marketing/PR firms like Ogilvy & Mather, which in turn have numerous corporate clients with a vested interest in shaping federal policies. Whitman is a veteran of the Clinton era and when making television appearances continues to be identified for work he did almost a decade earlier.

Other lobbyists combine the job of lobbying and public relations by stepping in front of the TV camera. When AIG was failing, Bernard Whitman, whose consulting firm worked for AIG 'as it responds to ongoing marketplace developments', appeared on news programmes,[51] where this was not revealed, to comment that AIG should not be allowed to fail. Viewers would have assumed he was a neutral expert. Two other experts fulfilled similar media roles, without revealing they were being paid by AIG to advocate AIG's position.

The second, and more serious problem, is that the process of selling dreams may make failure more likely. In January 2010, three economists – Deniz Igan, Prachi Mishra and Thierry Tressel – at the International Monetary Fund published a paper called 'Fistful of Dollars: Lobbying and the Financial

Crisis'.[52] In it, they found a correlation between the amount banks spend on lobbying and the risks they take with securitization of their loan books. They also have faster-growing mortgage loan portfolios, poorer share performance and larger loan defaults.

The economists selected 33 pieces of banking regulation that were the result of lobbying, and which lessened the oversight of banks. 'Our analysis suggests that the political influence of the financial industry can be a source of systemic risk', they wrote. To avoid bankrupt banks pitching us into financial crises, they added, we need to monitor lobbying more closely.

Influence isn't always bad, but it's never innocent. Just as off-balance-sheet 'special purpose entities' obscured Enron's true financial position, the influence that powerful companies exert behind the scenes sometimes creates an atmosphere of compliance and approval for unwise business practices. Sometimes, those practices can in turn obscure the rottenness at the heart of the businesses involved.

When we discover what has been going on, briefly, we are outraged. But the skilled people who upsell the precarious dreams of their fit-to-bust employers and clients work a seven-day week – and they know that soon enough, most of us are ready to be lied to again.

Chapter Four
Modern Rambos

Superman: Easy, miss. I've got you.
Lois Lane: You've got me? Who's got you? **(SUPERMAN, 1978)**

In an increasingly celebrity-obsessed culture, Nell Minow, founder of analysts the Corporate Library, has testified before the US Congress about how our adulation of chief executive officers (CEOs) seems to be a one-way street: heads they win, tails we lose.

'[For] CEOs, it's a very cozy negotiation with the directors they pick themselves', she told ABC News in the United States.[53] 'And those directors are writing a check on somebody else's bank account. And so they're very, very, very generous, and sometimes those directors are CEOs themselves, who are interested in paying this CEO a lot of money so they can go back and say, "Look, this is the new standard."'

Few of us refuse to be admired, and few of us refuse to have that admiration demonstrated with a $15 million golden hello, a yearly wage between $50 and $120 million, plus $1.22 million to redecorate our office, as former Merrill Lynch chairman and CEO John Thain had.

The CEO-as-celebrity causes problems that pop up all over this book: a tendency to be believed when they're wrong (or telling lies), an inflexibility because we either volunteer to (or they insist that we) do things their way. It encourages rash changes of direction and ego-driven growth strategies. Often they focus on pleasing groups who will make the maximum noise in their support: the media, analysts, shareholders.

Also, they have groups dedicated to pleasing them. The more terrifying CEOs often have employees dedicated to pleasing them without their knowledge. One acquaintance has the job, when her CEO visits, of making sure that every room he visits has the correct things in it: the right bottle of water, the correct lighting, the exact same buffet food, right down to the condiments. He has never, to her knowledge, expressed a preference for them, but providing them a couple of times a year has become a full-time job for her. Maybe by now he just assumes that everybody's room comes with chicken satay in the corner.

This makes it necessary to create a sort of anti-story: he's so extraordinary that he is just like us. When Bill Gates was the CEO of Microsoft, at the height of his personal fame and wealth (before he very successfully channelled it into his Foundation), the story regularly repeated by a fawning media was that, despite his exceptional qualities, Bill always flew economy class. At the time the UK's most popular technology newspaper, read by more than 100,000 people a week, asked if any readers, or the colleagues of any readers, or anyone in any company that any of the readers had ever worked for, had ever seen Bill on a flight. Bearing in mind that the technology business involves continuously flying to the same locations for conferences (at which Gates would often be the keynote speaker), it's surprising that no one had ever seen Bill, squished up in a little seat, working on his PowerPoint.[54]

The financial crisis has shown CEOs in an unflattering light. Often literally: peering up at politicians during committee sessions in Washington and London, flanked by their lawyers, or being jostled along the street by photographers on their way to court.

Anyone who has been around a modern large-company CEO will have observed that, often, they live in the sort of palatial bubble that royalty used to enjoy. It's not often that business writers get to use the word 'commode', but delighted journalists and outraged taxpayers boggled when the shopping list for Thain's Merrill Lynch office redecoration were revealed. When we looked closely at where the redecoration money went, $35,000 of this was famously spent on an antique 'commode on legs'. Thain had put a toilet in the middle of his office? Busy, busy man.

There's a more important point than the rock-star treatment. Many observers point out that the power that is thought to reside with shareholders actually rests with the CEO – especially if the CEO has the aura of a superman. The board, the employees and the investors are not able or are unwilling to rein in a rogue CEO. In *The Economics of Innocent Fraud*, the economist J K Galbraith comments that 'Managers, not the owners of capital, are the effective power in the modern enterprise... No one should be in any doubt.

Shareholders – owners – and their alleged directors in any sizeable enterprise are fully subordinate to the management.'

This has some negative effects. The second-worst is that we follow their bad decisions. Worst of all is that they follow their bad decisions.[55]

Chainsaw *Al Dunlap vs Sunbeam*

Albert J Dunlap has a special place in the league table of failed CEOs: whatever you think of his ideas about business, he is undoubtedly the one with the best nickname. He was known, to friends and foes alike, as 'Chainsaw',[56] and rather liked it. At one time it was a compliment – until, between 1996 and 1998, he took altogether too much of the chainsaw to Sunbeam Corporation, the failure that would destroy his reputation, along with the company.

Dunlap was delighted by his image as a tough guy. He even once posed for publicity shots for his book standing on his office desk, dressed as Rambo. His speciality was going into a company and doing whatever it took to fix things the way he liked it – and that usually meant firing a lot of people. This wasn't bad in itself – there are plenty of companies that have grown fat and complacent, and have refused to change because that's how they have always done things.

His first job as a CEO, in 1983, introduced the staff of Lily-Tulip Inc. to his methods: he fired 20 per cent of the staff, 40 per cent of the suppliers, 50 per cent of the management – including 11 of top 13 executives – and accomplished a dramatic turnaround, from a $1.8m loss in 1982 to a $22.6m profit by 1984. He slashed his way through several other companies before he arrived at Scott Paper Co., where he would make his reputation, in April 1994. Here, the cuts were even deeper: 35 per cent of employees – 11,200 redundancies – including 71 per cent of staff at headquarters, 50 per cent of managers, and 50 per cent of R&D on his way to generating a 225 per cent increase in the stock price – realizing $6.3 billion for investors when he sold the company to its biggest competitor 18 months later.

Though chiefly notorious among human resources departments for his towering rages, Dunlap also had many admirable qualities in a leader. Most of all, he got things done: whether his ideas were good or bad, they tended to happen. He was totally committed, and gave as much of himself as he demanded from his employees. He didn't fudge decisions, or believe in retaining the status quo for its own sake: a few weeks into his job at Sunbeam, he threw out all the filing cabinets in his office, because he had decided that 'there's nothing in them'. There are plenty of us who would have loved to have done the same thing. He was tailor-made for the wave of corporate cost-cutting in the 1980s and 1990s, becoming the high priest of the cult of downsizing: analysts said that he was a 'hero', a 'gift from heaven' when he cut away the fat from inefficient companies.

And for some companies, for a limited time, in some conditions, and in the eyes of some investors – he was a hero.

Dunlap's single-mindedness was his strength, but it was also his weakness. If you measured his success only by what he had earned for shareholders, and regarded every struggling company as ready for the chainsaw, he was the perfect CEO. And for those who believe that the job of the CEO is only to make money for shareholders, that's as complicated as it needed to be. As the long-time Chainsaw-watcher John A Byrne, who wrote the best account of Dunlap's career in his book *Chainsaw*, put it: 'He decried the more traditional view of the firm that said the corporations have many constituencies: stockholders, customers, employees and the communities in which they do business. To Dunlap, the only people who really mattered were those who put their money on the line.'

Shareholders matter most

The contrary view is that shareholders are, by their nature, short term. Realizing value in the short term might cripple your ability to compete next year, or the year after. Redundancies and disposals are expensive too, especially if the business has to grow again – by acquisition. Still, that's two sets of fees for investment banks. They didn't mind Chainsaw's methods too much.

By considering that his job was purely to create value for shareholders, Dunlap earned the admiration of those shareholders, and most of the analysts who reported to those shareholders. He wasn't so popular with the people whom he made redundant – he needed a 24-hour armed guard and on-call security for his house – but that was part of the job, and one he didn't shrink from. Say what you like about Big Al, he didn't mind p*ssing people off.

His ego helped him to push through change at a rate that had never been seen before with a curious lack of self-awareness that would have made him ridiculous – if he hadn't been so terrifying. In his autobiography (*Mean Business: How I Save Bad Companies and Make Good Companies Great*) he claimed to be 'a superstar in my field, much like Michael Jordan in basketball or Bruce Springsteen in Rock'n'roll'. A director who worked for him at Scott had a different interpretation: 'He repeated himself a lot, he became more overbearing and his ego was much more obvious.' He was fond of giving signed copies of his book to customers. Or screaming abuse at them. Or doing both in the same meeting.

You can accept the yelling, the insults, the aggression and most importantly the misery of thousands who were laid off, often in blue-collar towns, if there is no alternative. But when struggling Sunbeam hired him as CEO in July 2006, it was apparent to some that he wasn't going to be the saviour that he was in his own mind. Sunbeam certainly needed help: it had missed its sales targets five quarters in a row. It had diversified into all types of small electrical appliances and household goods. It had little direction, and it made everything from coffee pots to outdoor furniture.

Today's innovation: shouting

Dunlap appeared for his first day at work on 22 July 2006 and announced that 'The old Sunbeam is over today!' He proceeded to assault his board verbally for the entire day, insulting, belittling and chiding the other directors. 'The guy had an incredible capacity for elevating his voice and keeping it up there for hours and hours', James Wilson, head of human resources remembered. 'He screamed at us all morning.'

Most investors didn't mind, they liked the screaming. The day after he was hired, the stock went up 50 per cent. Just by turning up for work, Dunlap had made shareholders $6 per share. Four months later, he announced plans to eliminate 6,000 of the 12,000 employees and 87 per cent of the products, and to sell or consolidate 39 of 53 facilities and 18 of 26 factories. The changes, he said, would save $225m a year and cost $300m.

In 1997 he seemed to have worked his magic again: Sunbeam announced earnings of $187 million, higher than at any point in its history. The stock hit a maximum price of $52.

It was success, and the need to deliver on the success that he continued to promise, that broke Dunlap. He was a prisoner of his earlier achievements: his job was to cut, but, as a few analysts pointed out, Sunbeam's biggest problem wasn't that it was wasting too much money – it simply wasn't selling enough products. When you are cutting and reorganizing so savagely, it becomes harder in the short term to build long-term sales. Like a boxer who only trades in knockouts, Dunlap had only Plan A.

To execute his strategy (the management jargon 'execute' has never been more appropriate than it is here), he needed the support of major shareholders. And to do that, he needed to deliver a rise in the share price. And to do that, he needed to make the change that he, personally, had achieved in the balance sheet look better. Dunlap used two methods that aren't, to my knowledge, written up in management books.

According to the US regulator, Dunlap actually made Sunbeam look in worse trouble than it was in the short term. Afterwards the Securities and Exchange Commission (SEC) filed a complaint alleging that Dunlap had artificially depressed 1996 earnings so as to make 1997 earnings look spectacular – it alleged that $60 million of those 1997 earnings were fraudulent in this way. The complaint was never tested in public: Dunlap settled with the SEC, paid a fine, and is banned from being an officer of a public company.[57]

Rambo unravels

By the beginning of 1998, Dunlap's methods were causing Sunbeam, and not just its cowering employees, to unravel. To make sales figures he had encouraged the technique used as 'channel stuffing', where retailers committed to buy discounted product today for delivery later. It inflated sales, but meant that Sunbeam products were sitting in Sunbeam warehouses across the United States. Even though some of it hadn't even been paid for, Sunbeam was still recognizing the revenues on the balance sheet – a procedure that was, at best, on the outer limits of generally accepted practice. It fooled some credulous analysts, but Dunlap could not invent the cash flow that was needed to do things like pay the staff. Sales looked good, but Sunbeam was fast running out of cash.

He still might have made it through with his reputation, if it wasn't for the fact that shareholders loved him so. Analysts trusted him, almost unquestioningly, to make the numbers he promised. After the one-day boom in the share price, or even as it coasted higher to $20 or $30, Dunlap could have sold Sunbeam to one of its competitors and locked in the shareholder profit. He had done it before, many times. A CEO who knew how to grow sales gradually, rather than destroy jobs quickly, could have taken over.

But shareholders continued to buy his stock. As the price rose it became too expensive to sell off the rump of Sunbeam, so he had to stay and keep cutting nonsensically. When the board discovered that the company was, effectively, broke in June 1998 – and was going to make a one-quarter loss of $60 million – they belatedly summoned the courage to fire him. They sent not just the Chainsaw himself, but the whole method of running a company like a shooting gallery, into retirement.

Interviewed for *Business Week* in June 1998 in the immediate aftermath of Dunlap's firing, Edward E Lawler, a management professor at the University of Southern California, said that 'The need to do major downsizing is over. The opportunities to pick that kind of low-hanging fruit aren't as prevalent, and the second picking often requires different skills and methods than a Dunlap is known for. Clearly, his era has come and is going.'

'Organizations become committed to maximize short-term performance and to satisfy only short-term investors. Downsizing is taken to its illogical extreme, increasingly divorced from reality and economic sense, and increasingly informed by personal animus, ego and greed', Byrne wrote in *Chainsaw*. In Dunlap's famous hands the cult of downsizing had become corrupted by the obsessive need to keep doing it, even in the face of the evidence. Dunlap didn't get it: he had been rewarded all his life for firing people. In his final press conference, faced with criticism of his strategy and a falling share price, he did what he knew how to do: he promised another 5,100 layoffs.

As *Business Week* interviewee David M Friedson, CEO of Windmere-Durable Holdings Inc., described Dunlap's rise and fall as part of a special feature in 1998: 'He is the logical extreme of an executive who has no values, no honor, no loyalty, and no ethics. And yet he was held up as a corporate god in our culture. It greatly bothered me.'[58]

'Strip me naked, put me out on the streets, and I'm going to survive', Dunlap used to rant at anyone who would listen. Not this time, Al.

These people *Bear Stearns*

Bear Stearns had typified the high-risk, high-reward culture of global banking since the 1970s. Its managers built it up, but their arrogance ultimately broke it. True to form, the great men of Bear Stearns have been hurling insults ever since.

For example, Ace Greenberg, former CEO of Bear Stearns, commenting on his successor, Jimmy Cayne: 'I would not like to step in horsesh*t. So why would I stand around him? He's a lying f*cker.'[59]

Bear Stearns never did play nice. Every other bust company in this book committed suicide. Bear Stearns might be the only homicide. But, thanks to the way the firm behaved when it was alive, we aren't short of suspects if it was.

Since Bear Stearns was purchased for a fraction of its value by long-time rival J P Morgan in 2008, the testosterone that used to flood through the firm has spilled out. The former management are very angry: with each other, with the government, with its competitors. Not surprising: these great men of Wall Street, who built a firm of hard, nasty, unconventional, often uneducated, sometimes brilliant traders, lost their fortunes almost overnight. Most people agree that someone helped manufacture the run on Bear Stearns by spreading rumours about it that weren't true, but – as is the nature of this type of raid – no one who's talking knows who it was.

Suffering from PSD

'Ace' Greenberg, the man credited as the creator of the firm formerly known as The Bear, had a phrase for the people he employed to work there. He called them 'PSDs' – poor, smart, and with a deep desire to get rich. That's his background, and that was the type of hire that Bear Stearns looked for. While the other investment banks might have hired from top universities, Bear Stearns looked for raw talent. It hired people who were like the bosses. When Greenberg gave up the day-to-day running of the firm in 1993, Jimmy Cayne took over. Greenberg had discovered Cayne, who had started selling scrap metal, at a bridge tournament, and decided that anyone who could sell scrap could sell bonds.

In this, he was correct. Bear grew from a few hundred to a firm of 15,000 employees. The share price grew by 600 per cent when Cayne was CEO, and it branched out into asset management. Though it had diversified, it was still the roughest, toughest of all the big firms, and it was proud of its macho culture which, at one time, meant it didn't look too hard at whom it was doing business with.

In modern investment banking, the fates of all the banks are intertwined. They are your competitors, you may not personally like them, but you are locked in a deathly embrace with them, buying their products, using them as customers, and lending them money. It's this that makes the biggest firms too big to fail – unless, that is, you happen to be Bear Stearns.

In November 2007, Cayne wasn't having an easy time. His management style alternated Bear-style aggression with long periods away from the office, often playing bridge in tournaments, just like his mentor and predecessor. Following some extraordinary losses on two of the funds in its new asset management division, some commentators were beginning to ask whether the Bear's pressure-cooker management culture was too off the hook to handle a credit crisis. The *Wall Street Journal* had started the month with a 3,000-word feature alleging that Cayne was out of the office playing golf and bridge on 10 of the 21 workdays in July 2007 while his funds were collapsing,[60] and that he often didn't even take a cellphone on his trips. Cayne sent a memo to all staff, both denying the truth of the allegation and claiming that he was still 'intensely focussed' on the firm's business. Yet Bear had needed to bail out the two funds using $3 billion of its own money during a period when Cayne was noted in the news for his regular rounds of golf in New Jersey – which had sent exactly the opposite message to worried investors.

After the profile, David Trone, an analyst at Fox-Pitt Kelton Cochran Caronia Waller, rated Bear Stearns a 'buy', while he encouraged clients to sell all other investment banks. His reasoning: the financial crisis meant that The Bear was an acquisition target. At the time, its share price was just over $100.

Two months later Cayne, damaged by the criticism, had been replaced by another of the freewheeling Bear Stearns management set: Alan Schwartz. And two months after that, Schwartz was in Palm Beach, Florida, at a conference when rumours started that Bear Stearns was having liquidity problems. The firm had $18 billion of capital in the bank, so, with hindsight, we know the rumours were false. But they didn't go away.

It's impossible to know where the rumours started. But anonymous Bear Stearns sources later told *Vanity Fair* reporter Bryan Burrough, who wrote a long investigative report of the collapse of Bear Stearns,[61] that they thought they were started by the banks' competitors; maybe more than one.

At the time, the rumours stuck. There were several reasons. The first was the recent trouble that Bear Stearns' gung-ho management had created: an investment bank having to bail itself out was an unprecedented sign that management didn't know what was going on under their noses, which made the rumours more credible. The second was the image of a CEO, refusing to comment, in Palm Beach. This was a crisis! The third was the moment: with a series of write-downs and write-offs, modern banking was starting to creak. Investors were looking for the first sign of collapse. Investors who believed the rumours sold Bear Stearns (presumably some of whom had bought into it at double the price the previous November, hoping for an acquisition). Bear's plunging share price, in the strange logic of Wall Street, gave other investors all the evidence they needed that they should sell too.

A run on the bank

On 10 March 2008, the rumours were leading the financial news. Hedge funds, spooked, were starting to withdraw their funds. All investment banks rely on 'repo' – having other banks guarantee to lend them money overnight, so that they stay solvent. It's a mutual pact.

By 13 March the pact was no longer mutual. Its cash reserves were down to $15 billion, and repo lenders were unwilling to put up their money, in case the bank went bust overnight. By the end of the week, Bear had to look for anyone who could lend it the odd $30 billion. In the end, there was only one party that could put Bear Stearns on life support: the US Federal Reserve.

That weekend, Bear Stearns unravelled. The government, having originally guaranteed the funds for 28 days, decided that its generosity would not last past the weekend. Every rival sent a team to see what was worth salvaging. With a 48-hour deadline – the deal had to be done by the time Australian markets opened for Monday trading, or Bear would be bust for sure – that meant there wasn't time to do due diligence on vast portfolios of risky loans. The only bank that was still, grudgingly, in the race at the end of the process was its neighbour, J P Morgan. The deal was eventually done: at $12 a share. It could have been worse – the original price was agreed at $2.

Morgan had originally been the firm most likely to acquire Bear Stearns in 2007, when the price would have been 10 times what it paid. Yet it almost didn't do the deal at all. When it looked closely at the way the firm was run, without the excitement and macho bravado of the daily trading, much of the business that Bear Stearns was doing at the behest of its piratical management looked rotten. Morgan's assessment of the assets that might go bad leapt from $120 billion to $220 billion when it looked closely at the books. Burrough quotes an unnamed executive, who read an article about Bear Stearns management in the 16 March *New York Times*[62] – which was deadline day: 'That article certainly had an impact on my thinking. Just the reputational aspects of it, getting into bed with these people', he said.

The article dwelt on the wisdom of saving 'these people' – the management of a bank that had gambled and lost on sub-prime mortgages, and had even tried to dump its toxic assets on unsuspecting customers. But the meat and potatoes of the analysis centred on whether a firm that was managed in this fashion was ethically worth saving; it said:

> But why save Bear Stearns? The beneficiary of this bailout, remember, has often operated in the gray areas of Wall Street and with an aggressive, brass-knuckles approach. Until regulators came along in 1996, Bear Stearns was happy to provide its balance sheet and imprimatur to bucket-shop brokerages like Stratton Oakmont and A. R. Baron, clearing dubious stock trades.

When you so enjoyed the reputation for being the toughest, then the guys you used to beat up enjoy your comeuppance much more. The article quoted William A. Fleckenstein, president of Fleckenstein Capital: 'Why not set an example of Bear Stearns, the guys who have this record of dog-eat-dog, we're brass knuckles, we're tough?' he asked.

Fleckenstein got his wish.[63]

Mr Crapner *Ratners*

You don't have to scream and shout to make bad decisions. At the Institute of Directors (IoD) on Pall Mall, there's a small exhibition of historical documents celebrating famous events in the 107-year history of the organization. While much of the display celebrates the almost-famous and the great people whom you can't quite place until you read the caption, there's one part of the board that is immediately familiar to most of the members: the day that the entrepreneur hero of British business in the 1980s, and the world's biggest jeweller, inspired the phrase 'to do a Ratner'.

Compared to some of the disastrous, idiotic or criminal behaviour in this book, the collapse of Ratners is more of a farce. But it's a farce that shows how, when the CEO-as-hero forgets that customers aren't there to be laughed at, they will remind him.

On April 23 1991, Gerald Ratner made a £500 million joke.[64] At the IoD Annual Conference at the Albert Hall, Ratner was booked to make a speech. As one of the business stars of the greed-is-good decade he had taken on his family jewellers, in which he had started in 1966 aged 15, and made it into the world's biggest chain of jewellery shops. He owned 2,000 shops on two continents. He was earning £500,000 a year as chief executive and chairman and had houses in central London and Bray, and holidayed with the smart set in Barbados. He ate lunch with Margaret Thatcher at 10 Downing Street. He travelled by helicopter.

He was, in short, a bit flash. By 1991, he was trying to lose the image, because he knew that the reputation of Ratners – a bit cheap, slightly tacky, a supermarket for trinkets – would soon slow down his growth. Ratner had never truly been accepted as part of the Establishment, and his methods were beginning to change.

His 1990 results, released on the day of the speech, showed a company that was fighting hard in a recession but had still made profits of £112 million. £1 in every £3 spent on jewellery in the UK was spent at Ratners. He was number two in the US market, and growing fast there. Ratners, and its boss, seemed to be adjusting to the new environment.

'Gone are the days of losing up to £1,000 a night playing poker with Michael Green and Charlie Saatchi, wearing a gold ear-ring to shareholders' meetings, and issuing paper to fund more and bigger acquisitions as though it were recyclable', the *Independent on Sunday* wrote two days before his speech.[65] 'A sign of his own new respectability is that he in turn has been made a non-executive director of Norweb, one of the electricity generating companies.'

Ratner's rise had a direct cost. Ratners had debts equal to 70 per cent of its market value. Shares had to keep rising, and so shareholders needed to know that he could do more than sell trinkets. Sceptical investors needed to know that Ratner's magic touch worked in a different environment – represented by the not-flash IoD at the Albert Hall.

Old jokes are the best

Ratner had carved out a career as a public speaker with a neat line in self-denigration; he played the underdog, the boy-made-good, well. But it wasn't the genuine humility that a new breed of 'ethical' CEOs, like Anita Roddick of the Body Shop, was touting. The new generation stressed the need for respect for customers, the new discipline of corporate social responsibility, and that the CEO of a public company works for the shareholders. Ratner, in this context, was beginning to sound old-fashioned.

His 1980s business model had been wildly successful. Ratners had transformed from a dusty old chain of failing shops into a two-continent success by recognizing that jewellery, for most young people, wasn't a treasured family possession any more. Some of his stock made customers cheerful because it was cheap, bought to go out, or go to work. When he spoke in public he would get his laughs by making fun of his products.

He was advised to cut this out for the more staid IoD audience and national press journalists by his PR guru Lynn Franks, one of the best in the business. She warned him that, in a recession, the mood of the public was changing towards the businesspeople whose profiteering had defined the boom years of the 1980s. He was making fun of his products: customers thought he was making fun of them. His wife Moira said that 'It's just not that sort of event'.

But his accountant, who had been with him almost since the beginning, said he should put the jokes back in. So he did.

At the conference he got laughs for both his best lines, including: 'We also do cut-glass sherry decanters complete with six glasses on a silver-plated tray that your butler can serve you drinks on, all for £4.95. People say, "How can you sell this for such a low price?" I say, "because it's total cr*p".'

He described a pair of earrings that sold for 99p, saying they were 'cheaper than a Marks & Spencer prawn sandwich but probably wouldn't last as long'.

The next day, the *Mirror* led with the headline: 'You 22 carat gold mugs'. The *Sun*, always more pithy, had 'Crapners'. Ratner's humiliation went on for months: customers deserted the stores, embarrassed to be seen with prawn-sandwich jewellery, or to give it as a present. Ratner estimates that the company lost £500 million of its value as a result. He eventually agreed to be photographed by the *Sun* holding a toy gun to his head while he apologized, a disgraced fat cat in a world that had changed around him.

He wasn't a fraud – in fact, he was quite the opposite. If anything, he was too frank about where his lifestyle came from.

But his colleagues considered Ratners a prisoner of its 'total cr*p' past. By October 1992, it was all over. The chairman that Ratner himself had recruited asked him to leave, and the board of the company that carried his name, and which he had inherited from his own father, agreed. In his autobiography, Ratner explains that: 'I kept thinking that it would soon be over and that people would forget about the speech, that they'd stop calling me Mr Crapner, and that the phrase "doing a Ratner" would disappear.' No such luck. Almost 20 years on, his every business move is still described as the latest scheme by the man who once described his products as total cr*p. Which, Ratner is keen to point out, he didn't. He said that one of his decanters was total cr*p – a distinction which the public, who don't fly around in a helicopter and lunch with the prime minster, still don't see as important.

The man who always paid *Clarence Hatry*

Some entrepreneurs are blamed for the failure of their company. Some are blamed for wider social problems: hard times in a city, the failure of a technology, or a dip in the economic cycle. Few have been blamed for causing a global economic depression, but Hatry is one of them. But, if you don't learn from your mistakes, you're doomed to keep repeating them until you do something big enough that they take your toys away from you.

Psychoanalyst Michael Maccoby points out that narcissistic leaders 'are often more interested in controlling others than in knowing and disciplining themselves. That's why, with very few exceptions, even productive narcissists do not want to explore their personalities.' His solution: get into analysis, before you do real damage.[66]

This advice comes too late for Clarence Hatry. Depending on whether you were one of his many friends or one of his even more numerous enemies, he was either the cause of the Wall Street Crash and the depression that followed, or an innocent stooge who has been unfairly blamed for it.

The first charge is stretching the point a bit. But he certainly wasn't innocent.

So perhaps the kindest thing that can have happened to Hatry, once one of the most famous businesspeople on the planet, is that – for most of us – he is entirely forgotten. Known as 'the man who always pays', Hatry paid for his own mistakes – founded in an unshakeable belief in the rightness of what he was doing – with his reputation and nine years' hard time in prison.

Hatry's life started uneventfully: at the outbreak of the First World War he was an insurance clerk in London. The war liberated his talent for building businesses, and created the cult of Hatry. He quickly became a forerunner for what we know today as private equity: a man who would buy businesses, reorganize them quickly, and sell them again. By 1921, aged 33, he was fabulously rich and a director of 15 corporations. At the time he considered retiring from business life to enjoy his rooftop swimming pool (the only one in London) and the ownership of the largest yacht in British waters. He was also a popular hero: many of his swashbuckling business deals had the common touch, whether it was a small loans company which would help the middle classes better themselves, or even the first railway station photo booths.

Hatry was an innovator too. He encouraged English towns and cities to issue bonds to finance development. Although an outsider, he was the equal of the big banks in the primitive trade of financial engineering.

Unlike most of the CEOs in this book, Hatry was even good at failure: when his business empire failed in 1924 (Hatry's second bankruptcy), he pawned his wife's jewellery and borrowed the money to pay back his investors. He somehow managed to turn a large crash into a success story, and was soon putting together the biggest deal of all: United Steel companies. The merger would be worth £40 million – about half a billion today – but Hatry needed a bridging loan to pull it together. The Bank of England, as well as Lloyds Bank, refused to give it to him. Hatry needed to raise money quickly, and was caught guaranteeing loans from two different banks with the same bond certificates so that his deal would not fall apart.

A trial followed, at which he was sentenced to 14 years in Brixton Prison. He served nine, before being released to spend the rest of his days in the book trade – where, by his own admission, 'I knew I was engaging in an industry in which there were no fortunes to be made.'

Not by Hatry's standards: he still managed to buy stakes in 20 book stores and publishing companies.

Hatry's crash

Hatry was not an uncommon swindler at the time. In its coverage of the trial on 30 December 1930, *Time Magazine* pointed out that Hatry was heir to a great British tradition of business failure. Forgotten names like Jabez Spencer Balfour (whose Liberator Building Society collapsed with debts of £50,000,000) and Alfred Carpenter ('under whose able mismanagement' the Charing Cross Bank failed with losses of £8,500,000) spoke of a certain overconfidence in the speculators of the time.

Hatry's special notoriety was due to the scale and the timing of his final, and biggest, bust. When the Bank of England declared that his company was bankrupt on 20 September 1929, it triggered a collapse in his empire that left his companies with losses of $67,500,000, shared among 27 banks. It was, at the time, the biggest bankruptcy in British history, and disaster for both the stock market and the banking establishment.

Worse followed: Hatry had confessed to fraud on the same day as the shares in his company were suspended. Some investors panicked. Less than two weeks later, the Wall Street Crash was in full swing. Many consider the wobble in the stock market that began with the unmasking of 'The Man Who Always Pays' as 'The Man Who Is Going to Prison' as the tipping point from boom to bust. He became emblematic of the unwise speculation and sense of entitlement that created the Crash. His friends, who continued to campaign for him from prison, never accepted this to be true. They even published a pamphlet in his defence in 1931, preserved in the British Library, called 'The Hatry Case: Eight Current Misconceptions', which listed the stock prices of the London Stock Exchange's major corporations before and after his arrest, to show that there was no short-term effect on share prices.[67]

The great economist of the period John Kenneth Galbraith gives Hatry less credit. In his history of the Wall Street Crash (*The Great Crash*, 1929), Galbraith says that 'although his earlier financial history had been anything but reassuring, Hatry in the twenties built up an industrial and financial empire of truly impressive proportions... his expansion owed much to the issuance of unauthorized stock, the increase of assets by the forging of stock certificates, and other equally informal financing.'

Hatry seems, with hindsight, to have acquired a better appreciation of his flaws in prison than his friends did, who continued to find him blameless. He consciously cut corners, fuelled by faith in his ability to make things turn out right: as a man who got things done in the stuffy world of 1920s high finance, supporters looked the other way through two bankruptcies, and continued to find him blameless even after he admitted to a fraud worth millions of pounds. He didn't cause the Wall Street Crash alone, but he was timely evidence that much of the roaring twenties had been built on speculation. Investors realized that, once you looked closely, much of the value of the stock market was based in trust of people like Hatry. As long as everything kept growing, he was the man who made it happen. When the bubble popped, he was one of the men who made that happen too.

Hatry, a slight and unhealthy-looking man – even when he held glamorous parties around that rooftop pool in Mayfair, or on that largest yacht in British waters – retained the appearance of Clark Kent while behaving like Superman. His investors paid too much attention to image, and too little to his track record of loading successful businesses with debt until they collapsed. Galbraith treats him as an example of egotistical rashness that hypnotizes those of us who want people like him to succeed: 'Hatry was one of those curiously un-English figures with whom the English find themselves periodically unable to cope', was his diagnosis.

Heads they win, tails we lose

People like Al Dunlap, Bernie Ebbers and Jeff Skilling demonstrate the dark side of modern management theory. Look on them, ye mighty, and despair: we created managers with charisma and the ability – consciously or unconsciously – to impose their will on others.

This they do. In many cases of fit-to-bustness, there's a lot of management direction, straight from the top, that's matched by an absence of ethical or practical questioning from below. We are far more willing to blindly obey than we would care to admit.

In this case the mission, embodied in the CEO, has supplanted the mission embodied in the company. Ideally, they are the same. Practically, the mission becomes inseparable from the personality of the CEO tasked to perform it.

When a CEO's tenure lasts years, or decades, and the CEO is sufficiently self-aware to rein in destructive tendencies, this may be positive. Employees can use the personality of the CEO as a shorthand to find their way through the problems of decision making: a sort of 'What would the boss do if he were me?' way to manage. That, however, is idealistic.

Even in this best of all possible worlds, there are problems. The first is that the CEO was hired to manage in one situation, and the situation may have changed – but the boss, rewarded for a set of behaviours which are no longer appropriate, has not.

The CEO also has a conflicting set of incentives. He needs to keep his job, and that means delivering short-term growth, sometimes at the expense of long-term stability. He needs to look good, and in times of strife that can mean shutting down dissent. He needs validation, and that might mean appointing a management team of yes-men, including outside directors, who serve at his whim.

Power and money distort our thinking, especially for a narcissistic CEO. The modern chief executive has more power, and is better rewarded, than management has ever been.

Not surprising, then, that while we rejoice in management theory that promotes consensus, sharing, continuous learning and humility, we find an alarming number of CEOs who are arrogant and overbearing. In the short term this can be incredibly effective, as Al Dunlap showed. But they are compensated at levels which bear no relation to the value they create.

Learn to obey

Management coaches David Dotlich and Peter Cairo identify destructive CEO behaviour in their book *Why CEOs Fail*.[68] They pinpoint 11 different failings, but the first is arrogance: crossing the line between fighting for what you believe in (good) to fighting no matter what (bad); or deciding what's correct before, rather than after, hearing other points of view. The symptoms are a diminished capacity to learn, a refusal to be accountable, resistance to change and the inability to recognize your limitations.

They also point out that CEOs are more vulnerable to derailing behaviour. 'The higher you go in an organization, the less likely other people are to tell you about your failure-producing characteristics. CEOs' jokes are funnier, their insights are brighter, and they are routinely considered the fount of all wisdom.'

To reduce the effect of this behaviour, CEOs need to be able to listen. There is plenty of evidence, however, that an all-powerful CEO, especially the type of hero CEO that the soap operatic nature of 21st-century capitalism often demands, is in post partly because of an ability to manipulate subordinates. To understand how, we have to examine the work of social psychologist Professor Stanley Milgram.

Milgram performed one of the most famous, and disturbing, experiments in modern sociology. In it, a subject was asked to help perform an experiment. The learner, whom the subject hears but does not see, has to answer questions – which he consistently gets wrong. An authority figure directs the subject to administer electric shocks to the learner, increasing in intensity. The learner screams in pain and begs the subject to stop. The experiment is a fake, but the subject thinks that he or she is giving near-fatal shocks, for no other reason than that an authority figure assures the subject that it is not his or her responsibility.

Two-thirds of people who acted as subjects were willing to give the imaginary learner a 450 Volt shock. Milgram concluded that:

> Ordinary people, simply doing their jobs, and without any particular hostility on their part, can become agents in a terrible destructive process. Moreover, even when the destructive effects of their work become patently clear, and they are asked to carry out actions incompatible with fundamental standards of morality, relatively few people have the resources needed to resist authority.[69]

In the face of this test of obedience, it's hardly surprising that many employees are willing to falsify sales, fake reports or cheat customers to help a powerful

CEO achieve targets for the company. Or is it? Milgram's experiment took place in private, in a closed environment, without an audience. The subjects, he reasoned, put aside morality and acted as 'agents' of authority for that time. Yet we go home from work every night. Few of us want to feel we are defined by our jobs. Other people would see us breaking the rules. We can complain to HR, or in extreme circumstances, to the police. We can quit.

So it's a backhanded tribute to a man like Bernard Madoff, for example, that he can encourage a group of employees to help him commit fraud over a period of decades. A CEO like this is indeed special, just not in a good way, and the power to make us conform to bad – in this case criminal – behaviour shows how much of our ethical code is potentially shaped by our employers.

Don't ask questions

While our trust in authority figures such as politicians, the police or the church has declined, the relative importance of the corporate structure around us has increased in power. It can make us rich. It gives us status. It can make people admire us. Some of this has been passed to it from other traditional power structures. We recognize that. We not only have more to gain, we are taught that CEOs have a rare and unusual brilliance. Often we are told that the brightest people no longer go into academia or government, but into business. So we learn that they are most often correct. We learn to question managers less, even when we don't understand them.

Also, the way in which the CEO transmits the message is more immediate and more sophisticated. Once the CEO was remote. Now the company meeting, the e-mail to all staff, the video message or even internal company radio and TV broadcasts are commonplace. The CEO lives inside our computer. According to one recent paper: 'We suggest that people high in political skill not only know precisely what to do in different social situations, but exactly how to do it with a sincere, engaging manner that disguises any ulterior motives and inspires believability, trust and confidence, and renders the influence attempt successful.'[70]

For Danielle Beu and Ronald Buckley,[71] in a paper entitled 'This is war: How the politically astute achieve crimes of obedience through the use of moral disengagement', this can lead directly to immoral acts: 'leaders can frame the employees' view of the situation so that employees believe what they are doing is ethical or that they have no other choice but to obey'. This is particularly prevalent in the personalized style of leadership: 'Personalized leaders demand their followers' unquestioning loyalty and obedience. Followers surrender their power and become dependent on the leader to the point that failure to comply with the leader's requests is unthinkable.'

We're also selected at the first stage for our capacity for obedience. At interview we strive to show how aligned we are with the goals of the company. Only those of us who succeed get hired. The ability to get the job done is favoured over the ability to ask why we're doing the job in the first place.

The potential for unwise obedience extends not just to the little people, like us, but to those who are employed specifically to check the power of the leader, to ask those questions. That might mean auditors or legal counsel, but also this means the outside, or non-executive, directors. Every board has them, and nominally they are there to apply a brake on executive decision making, an alternative view. But an outside director is usually the appointment of the CEO. They are paid by the company. Their knowledge of the company is sketchy compared to the intimate involvement that the executive directors have. The story of WorldCom, for example, shows how easy it is to manipulate the information they see.

One recent study shows that, when the CEO is involved in the selection process, outside directors are more likely either to be yes-men or to have a conflict of interest.[72] When the CEO is involved in selection, outside reactions to new appointments are also reduced. This implies that CEOs use their involvement to 'reduce pressure from active monitoring'.

In short: as soon as they sit down, outside directors become inside directors.

Money is power

If the measurement of CEO accomplishment is CEO pay, then this generation has seen managers who are approximately 10 times as good as they used to be. The Institute for Policy Studies monitors executive pay. In 1980, the average CEO was paid 42 times the earnings of the average worker. By 1990, it was 107 times. By 2000, in the midst of the stock market boom, it was 525 times. By 2008 that had declined to 319 times, but still a dramatic increase in less than 30 years.

In the United States, AFL-CIO analysis shows that the average pay of a CEO for an S&P 500 company in 2009 was $9,246,697.[73] On one hand, this looks healthy, because only just over $1 million is basic pay, while almost $5 million is made up of stock and stock options. One of the reasons that CEOs are paid dramatically more than they used to be is that they are now directly incentivized by being awarded chunks of the company that they run.

The change in the US habit of awarding stock options came in 1993, when companies were allowed to expense the stock options they awarded to executives. For fast-growing technology companies, who needed to hang on to cash but wanted ambitious managers, this was ideal.

Paying the CEO with stock options solved two problems at once. You could reward the bosses by literally giving them a chunk of what they had created, while in accounting terms 'pretending that nothing of value had changed hands', in the words of economist Joseph Stiglitz.[74] Stock options were wildly popular in the dot-com boom: in 2001, 80 per cent of the compensation of American corporate managers involved stock options of some type. In that year, if Microsoft had been forced to give the dollar value of the options it awarded to staff, its profits would have dropped by one-third. Intel would have made one-fifth of the profit that it made, and Yahoo! would have made a net loss.

In the opinion of Stiglitz – and many others who have gasped at the greed, anger and arrogance of the failed-company CEOs they watch on the evening news – 'the vaunted energy and creativity of the 1990s would eventually be directed less and less into new products and services, and more and more into ways of maximizing the executives' gains at the unwary investor's expense... the executives are being paid too much partly because it isn't widely known how much they are really being paid.'

His argument is that we have the stock option incentive backwards. In a stock market boom, most of the value of the increase in a company's share price has little to do with the actions of management, and so you are rewarding good managers and bad managers equally. Even if you find that hard to swallow, he adds that many of these packages are asymmetric: when the markets were going up, then executives argued in favour of being compensated with stock. When the markets were going down, they argued that they should get bonuses for achieving better-than-average performance, even when the share price falls. 'It was a classic heads-I-win-tails-you-lose arrangement', he writes. 'Executive pay depended on stock prices in the short run, and in the short run it was easier to improve the appearances of profits than to increase the profits.'

Power and influence aren't bad things in a CEO – a boss who has no power and no influence would be far worse. But when they are used to serve the

CEO rather than the group, it creates a problem. Narcissistic CEOs can create dramatic success in the short term. By definition, their self-control is weak – but often they have appropriated so much of the power inside their companies that other directors, auditors and shareholders are unable, or unwilling, to control them too.

The great football manager and self-diagnosed big-head Brian Clough, the model of a high-achieving narcissist, once described how he dealt with people who disagreed with him: 'We talk about it for twenty minutes. And then we decide I was right.'

Chapter Five
All together now

I'll have what she's having. OLD WOMAN, LISTENING TO FAKED ORGASM IN DELI (*WHEN HARRY MET SALLY,* 1989)

Sometimes an entire culture gets infected with an idea so enticing that it seems too good to be true. Then it turns out that it was too good to be true after all.

Even when there's no terrifying chief executive officer (CEO) demanding obedience, we have a limited ability to question the conventional wisdom. We're remarkably good at finding consensus when the status quo has created success.

Dave Arnott of the American Management Association[75] warns that too many employers today show all the features of a cult: they inspire devotion, they have charismatic leadership, and they separate you from your community (he points out that this, the accepted definition of a cult, is functionally identical to the criteria for *Fortune Magazine*'s list of Best Places to Work: Sense of purpose, Inspiring leadership, Knockout facilities).

People who join cults make bad decisions, not because they are stupider than the rest of us, but because the cult destroys their ability to perform critical thinking. When your employer satisfies larger parts of your life – providing a crèche and shops, telling you when you can take a holiday, providing many of the measures against which you measure your self-worth – it occupies a higher position of trust (you give your employer your children to take care of all day?) than most of your friends.

When your individualism is subordinated to the group, there are some positive effects: a sense of community and teamwork, the idea of self-sacrifice to help your co-workers, a sense of collective pride.

The cost is groupthink. A community, a group, a company or a country sleepwalks to disaster – all the while congratulating themselves on their wonderful insight.

Frozen assets *Iceland*

When West Ham United football club found new owners in June 2006, the traditional East London club gave many observers their first exposure to a new type of financial speculator. While other sporting clubs were being snapped up by wealthy Arab investors or US corporate raiders, West Ham confused its fans by announcing that the new owner was an Icelandic billionaire brewer and bank owner called Bjorgolfur Gudmundsson. His chairman, Eggert Magnusson, was the CEO of a biscuit-manufacturing company, and promised European Champions League football in five years.

If the fans worried that the Icelanders had big ideas and small wallets, they were quickly convinced otherwise. The club quickly started to acquire players. When Brazilian forward Adriano became available, West Ham enquired, politely, how much he wanted to be paid. Inter Milan said £110,000 a week. After consulting with the owner, Magnusson gave the go-ahead, to the astonishment of everyone on both sides of the deal.[76]

This was the Icelandic way. Spend big, buy assets, borrow more money, buy more assets. Icelandic companies bought large chunks of UK retail, including the giant toy store Hamleys. They paid top price, but it didn't seem to matter when the price of the assets kept rising – even if that was partly because the Icelandic investors were in the market for them. Around the time that West Ham was negotiating for the asset named Adriano, Iceland's banks had $140 billion in other assets, 50 times what Icelanders owned in 2002. The stock market was up by a factor of nine in four years.

When the bubble popped and the banks that were buying the assets plunged into receivership, Icelanders woke up to the reality that the investments were certainly unsustainable, and some may even have been criminal. Many Icelanders had gone to work in the financial sector, and were now redundant. Others looked at the collapsing currency, wondered how to pay debts that they had in yen or Swiss francs, and asked: how did this happen? It's a question that we can only half answer, even now.

Over their heads

In the history of financial mass hysteria we've had a few fixed points: the South Sea Bubble (later in this chapter), the Tulip Mania (next chapter) or the Wall Street Crash. While they are all examples of how dangerously irrational crowds can be, we also assume that they happened because that was how things were in those days. The thing about international banking in the global economy, many people would have told you in 2006, is that risks are securitized – parcelled up and sold to other banks – and that capital flows to the places where the return against risk is best. Which meant that reckless banking would be spotted early, and reckless bankers wouldn't attract capital. The global financial system would be self-regulating.

This doesn't begin to explain the craziest investment bubble in the history of the planet: the spree that Iceland's three bloated banks went on between 2001 and 2008.[77] The investment bubble they created almost bankrupted the country, has plunged it into severe recession, and has depleted the pensions of Icelanders by up to 25 per cent. At one time Iceland had foreign debt of €160,000 per person. It owed around 900 per cent of its gross domestic product (GDP).

Iceland's banks were deregulated late: in 2001. The country, with a GDP of around €20 billion, was an unlikely seat of financial wizardry. Its main industries were fishing and aluminium smelting, and although it had an educated workforce, there simply weren't enough of them with banking expertise to start a financial sector. That's what you might assume, anyway.

Yet the three banks, Glitnir, Landsbanki and Kaupthing, profited from the global boom by borrowing previously unimaginable sums on the capital markets. The 'carry trade', in which money from low-interest-rate economies is borrowed and lent to high-interest-rate economies, meant that Iceland attracted a lot of investment.

The heroes of Iceland's banking revolution, such as Lyour Gudmundsson and Agust Gudmundsson of Kaupthing, or Bjorgolfur Thor Bjorgolfsson and Bjorgolfur Gudmundsson, who owned Landsbanki, were the heroes of the business pages. Their apparent financial wizardry, based on almost no experience of banking or international business, was delivering spectacular returns for large and small investors alike. Half a million foreigners – more than the population of Iceland – had opened accounts with Icelandic banks. Many local councils in the UK invested in Iceland's banks, a sum equal to about 5 per cent of the UK's Council Tax in 2008.

Iceland's population had their own carry trade going: they were borrowing in yen and Swiss francs, where interest rates were low, to buy houses and expensive cars on the cheap. The higher the krona climbed, the more they could afford. Suddenly, everyone was an entrepreneur.

Drowning, not waving

As the banking business ran hotter, not everyone was convinced. In January 2008, as the credit crunch was beginning to affect the liquidity of global financial markets, Landsbanki asked Professor Willem Buiter and Professor Anne Sibert, two London-based economists, to investigate the stability of the banking system. In July 2008, they presented the paper at a meeting of Iceland's Central Bank, economists and academics. Their conclusion was straightforward: 'This business model for Iceland is not viable.'[78]

With hindsight, the argument was obvious. As long as asset prices continued to rise, and debt was freely available, there was little risk. But when the party stops, banks globally need a lender of last resort to guarantee that our deposits with that bank are safe. Without this, the minute we get nervous, we all want our money back, and the bank collapses; alternatively, if other banks don't want to lend to a weak bank with no lender of last resort, then that bank is out of business. The lender of last resort is, usually, the Central Bank.

But the bloated banks of Iceland had so far outstripped the capacity of the Central Bank to guarantee their massive debts that there was no last resort in a crisis. Once nervous investors or lenders knew, there would be either a run on the bank or a liquidity crisis. The result of either would be the same.

'It was absolutely obvious, as soon as we began to study Iceland's problem, that its banking model was not viable', the authors wrote. 'We are pretty sure this ought to have been clear in 2006, 2004 or 2000. The Icelandic banks' business model and Iceland's global banking ambitions were incompatible with its tiny size and minor-league currency.'

The Icelanders asked that the paper be kept private. If more people knew about its contents, they reasoned, the dire consequences that it predicted would immediately come to pass.

Collapsing banks

The secrecy didn't delay the end for long. The end of the Icelandic banking dream – the fastest expansion of banking anywhere in the history of the world – was brutal and sudden. In the global liquidity crisis that followed the collapse of Lehman Brothers, Iceland's banks suddenly looked like a very bad bet indeed. On 5 October, Iceland's prime minister told the country there was no need for emergency measures to protect the banks. A day later, the Financial Services Authority was empowered to take over the running of banks if it proved necessary. The government guaranteed the savings of retail depositors. By 7 October, Landsbanki and Glitnir were in receivership and nationalized, to be followed two days later by Kaupthing. By 19 November the government, without anything like the reserves needed to make a European- or US-style injection of funds, had agreed loans of $4.6 billion from the International Monetary Fund (IMF), and $6.3 billion from the UK, Germany and the Netherlands.

The government had tried to peg the krona, Iceland's currency, against the euro on 6 October. Humiliatingly, it had to abandon the peg after two days. The government's peg was 131 krona to the euro. When it floated, it was worth less than half.

The aftermath has been ugly. Iceland has traditionally been a stable society, built on close ties between its inhabitants, a sense of equality and communal living. At the time of writing, the investigation into whether there was fraud, run by Member of the European Parliament (MEP) Eva Joly, is 'the largest investigation in history of an economic and banking collapse'. Gylfi Magnusson, Iceland's economy minister, posted a blog which admitted similarities between Iceland's banking system and failed US energy company Enron. In 2009, Iceland's economy contracted by 6.5 per cent.

Dr Jon Danielsson, who teaches economics at the London School of Economics – and whose offer to help the Icelandic government during the crisis was rejected – dismisses the two explanations offered most often by former bankers: that the banks were sound, just short of liquidity; and that the British government forced the collapse by using anti-terrorist legislation to guarantee deposits for UK savers.

Instead, Danielsson says that the banks were set up to take unwise risks from day one, echoing the idea that 'this ought to have been clear in 2006, 2004 or 2000'. 'The government had no understanding of the dangers of banks or how to supervise them', he says.[79]

The investigation is asking whether there was share ramping – the bank lending money to people to buy shares in the same bank. Kaupthing, several weeks before it collapsed, released a statement that 'Kaupthing's position is strong', based on the acquisition of a 5 per cent stake by a Qatari investor. Later it emerged that the stake was bought using a loan from Kaupthing.

In May 2010, Sigurdar Einarsson, former chief executive of Kaupthing, was listed on Interpol's website as 'wanted'. Investors accuse banks, banks accuse investors of causing the problem. Glitnir is accusing one of the investors to whom it lent money of 'siphoning out' cash to prop up the investments he bought, and has issued a $2 billion lawsuit to get the money back.

Exasperated Icelanders who aren't part of the blame and backstabbing forced out the government who presided over the disaster by demonstrating in January 2009. The Icelanders haven't lost their flair for community: a group organized a 1,500-person brainstorm in a sports stadium last winter, to try to overcome the sense of paralysis that has gripped the government as it tries to find the cash to pay its huge debts.[80] Participants for the brainstorm were selected at random from the voters' register. 'Everyone is waiting for something to happen. And we can't wait any longer. The only solution is to push up our sleeves and start working on what we want to do', said Halla Tomasdottir, CEO of Audur Capital, one of the organizers.

Former West Ham football club owner Bjorgolfur Gudmundsson, once Iceland's second-richest man, applied for bankruptcy protection at Reykjavik district court in July 2009. The former billionaire was $759 million in debt. West Ham has new owners, who don't pay £110,000 per week. They never made it to the Champions League.

An undertaking of great advantage
The South Sea Company

Bizarre get-rich-quick cults, like Iceland's descent into financial madness, are not a modern invention. In 1720 a London businessman set up 'A company for carrying on the undertaking of great advantage, but nobody knows what it is.'[81] He required £500,000 to undertake this great advantage, and he advertised that he was going to sell 5,000 shares at £100 each to investors. All you had to do was to come and see him at his office, leave a £2 deposit, and you would be rewarded with the opportunity to invest in a scheme that would pay you £100 per share per year. We know, from the best chronicle of this period in English commerce, that he opened his office for one day only: 'Crowds of people beset his doors, and when he shut up at three o'clock, he found that no less than one thousand shares had been subscribed for.' In one day, the businessman had made £2,000, in cash, by advertising that he had a good idea. That's worth almost £500,000 today.

This was only one of the 100 joint stock companies that were launched in a frenzy of entrepreneurialism that made the dot-com boom look like a school fete. In England in 1711, the public debt needed to be paid off. Instead of raising taxes in some way, the government of the day decided that they would use the new-found enthusiasm for global exploration and trade to raise cash. And so the South Sea Company was granted a monopoly of trade from the South Seas (what is now the coast of Latin America). Ordinary people, at least those with money to invest, were allowed to invest in a share of the company, and were promised spectacular profits if they did.

The nation was captivated by stories of inexhaustible gold and silver mines which would guarantee a dividend on the precious shares in the South Sea Company for a lifetime. As Mackay says in *Extraordinary Public Delusions*, 'everyone believed them to be inexhaustible, and that it was only necessary to send the manufactures of England to the coast to be repaid a hundredfold in gold and silver ingots by the natives'.

At the time, very few people knew better. The only news of the mines was brought back by the people who had visited the South Seas – who were, of course, employed by the South Sea Company, and who were, of course, the beneficiaries of any investment.

Awkward facts

They took the opportunity to leave out the part about how the Spanish controlled most of the territory (including the gold and silver) already, and that the opportunities for trade were non-existent. The South Sea Company was a success because everyone wanted a piece of it. It was one of the world's first stock bubbles, and it was also one of the most successful – if it is possible to have a successful bubble.

At that time the stock market was literally a market. There was a daily crush in Exchange Alley, as the 'jobbers' – a group of people who actually made the trades on behalf of the buyers and sellers – did their business. The stock in the South Sea company rose from £130 continuously until it hit £1,000 in August. At times it was possible to buy stock at one end of Exchange Alley, push through the crowds to the other end, and sell for an instant profit of 10 per cent.

What lessons can we take from this? The first is the power of enthusiasm. There simply wasn't enough South Seas stock to go around, so when other joint stock companies were launched, those who missed the first wave of investments bought into those. There was a company for 'encouraging the breed of horses in England, and of improving of glebe and church lands, and repairing and rebuilding parsonage and vicarage houses', for 'Improving of gardens', for 'Drying malt by hot air', for 'Extracting silver from lead' and for 'the art of making soap'. They all sounded like jolly good ideas, and so – even if they didn't sound quite as alluring as a gold mine in Latin America – hundreds of the middle classes sold their possessions to invest in them. Many bought 'Globe Permits': square pieces of card on which there was the seal of the Globe Tavern. Mackay again: 'The possessors enjoyed no other advantage from them than permission to subscribe at some future time to a new sail-cloth manufacture... these permits sold for as much as sixty guineas.' Sixty guineas: about £13,000 today.

The second is the ability of the human mind to jump straight from the origin to the conclusion. It is this that causes hundreds of untrained people to ignore the statistics on restaurant ownership that say that 9 out of 10 of them won't last a year, and to set up their own businesses. When we hear of a company that wants to extract silver from lead, we don't picture a group of people scratching their heads while they stare at a piece of lead, or a couple of crooks running off with our money – we imagine a pile of silver bars. We communicate by telling stories. Entrepreneur stories are stories of hope.

The third is that, at first, stock ownership can turn enthusiasm alone into profit for a few insiders, and we all want to be insiders. The first stockholders of the South Sea company did very well: not least because the price for their share of the company was that they were enthusiastic in public. Real insiders didn't, and as we will see still don't, have to do anything as vulgar as pay for their shares. One of these insiders, it was discovered later, was Mr Aislabie, the Chancellor of the Exchequer, the first in a long line of public officials whose oversight wasn't quite what it appeared.

We'll deal with bubbles, why we don't spot them, and why – even when we do – we still invest in them in more depth in the next section, but at a simple level enthusiasm alone can create the illusion of success in the short term, and that success is often held up as proof that the business idea is sound.

Just as start-up companies today will tell you how many people have registered their interest, or how many hits their website has had, or how many people have downloaded their software, or how many customers have purchased the loss-leading product, so any representative of the South Sea company in 1720 would have had only to show a doubter the crush in Exchange Alley.

And the fourth thing? With the price of stock in the South Sea Company into four figures, finally the voices that questioned whether there would ever be worthwhile trade with the South Seas (and whether the other joint stock schemes would ever create the fabulous dividends they promised) began to be heard. Like a hangover after a night of binge drinking, the euphoria departed even more swiftly than it built up.

The South Sea Company collapsed before the end of 1720. The fortunes of many wealthy Englishmen collapsed with it. The country's finances (remember, this was started with the noble aim of paying off the country's debts) were almost bankrupted too. Even the great Sir Isaac Newton lost, according to his niece, a sum equivalent to around £400,000 of today's money in the scheme.

And what was 'the undertaking of great advantage, but nobody knows what it is'? We will never know. Having pocketed his £2,000, the mystery businessman closed his doors, immediately sailed for France, and was never heard of again.

His spirit lives on, though: in the internet boom around the year 2000, one company issued stock on the basis that it would 'possibly invest in Internet related enterprises'. The stock traded at twice the value of the cash in its account – its only asset.

Astounding and momentous failure
General Motors

Some cults are creative, but wrong. Others seem to just get stuck: like GM.

In April 2007, before the credit crunch hit, it was already becoming obvious that it wasn't a question of if GM would survive, but how soon it would need to declare bankruptcy. Rival Toyota presented the keynote speech at the Advertising Research Foundation (ARF) in New York, the largest research conference in the United States. Why did a group of market researchers care about Toyota? Because it had used the innovative technique of asking what customers wanted, and actually providing it, to win market share from GM among customers who had always sworn they would only buy American.

Steve Sturm, Toyota group vice president (VP) for strategic research in North America, gave a list of examples in which US car manufacturers had failed, but the most surprising was GM's heartland – trucks. Toyota researchers had visited 'truck graveyards' to find out why old trucks were abandoned: when they found the first parts to rust through or break, they engineered their own products so that wouldn't happen. When truck drivers answered that they bought only American products, instead of giving up, the researchers kept probing until they had found what the owners considered to be the 'Americanness' of their truck. They discovered which drivers might want to switch, and which ones were most likely to set the trend – and then they marketed their efficient, well-made, low-cost trucks to them. The level of detail: Toyota found that GM was unconsciously irritating ranchers by making radios with small knobs on that they couldn't tune while wearing working gloves.

The result had been a long, slow decline in GM market share, and an equally long, slow improvement in Toyota's share. The owners who were fiercely loyal to GM were also practical. Their loyalty couldn't be bought, but it could be earned. And thanks to GM's long-running policy of encouraging its drivers to change their vehicle regularly, eventually they found their best customers were changing to Toyota.

GM had targeted young drivers – 25 per cent of the driving-age population today are under 30. That segment had a buying power of $2.3 trillion, but GM (and it wasn't alone in this) simply thought that they wanted a car that looked like their parents' car, but maybe a bit smaller. Instead, Toyota created a series of brands that – if you are out of that age range – you might not even know exists. Cars like the Scion weren't advertised on TV, and were specifically made not to look like your dad's choice – even though, for most buyers, it was a present, or at least the selection, of the mother or father. Scion has its own music label and clothing ranges. Four out of five buyers were new to Toyota, defecting from American brands.

GM was undone because the things that made it great didn't work anymore. And nobody was able to stop the decline.

Good for GM, good for the United States

GM had, for most of the 20th century, been great. In the 1950s, when Charles Wilson was CEO of General Motors, he was suggested as Secretary for Defense. He had to undergo a Senate vetting procedure. One of the questions: could he make a decision that was good for the government, but not good for GM?

'For years I thought that what was good for our country was good for General Motors, and vice versa', he said. He, and most others, couldn't separate the two economically.[82]

It's fitting that the crisis that plunged the United States into its worst post-war recession also did for GM: the company filed for Chapter 11 bankruptcy on 1 June 2009. It was the largest non-financial failure of the bust, just as it had arguably been the greatest beneficiary of the boom. For years GM was the United States' largest company: in the 1930s it was responsible for about 3 per cent of US GDP. As late as 2000, it was top of the Fortune 500, and even in 2007 only Wal-Mart and Exxon were bigger.

Unlike the banks though, GM was not too big to fail.

Over the past 30 years GM has managed to destroy hundreds of billions of dollars of shareholder value in many ways. There are hundreds of reasons that GM failed: spiralling pension costs, the power of the unions, the changing habits of Americans, the inability to produce products that worked outside its domestic markets, poor build quality, over-complicated management structures, a lack of appreciation of what was happening in the world outside Detroit all get a mention. In the 1930s, GM had 42 per cent market share. The fact that its decline took 30 years at least to result in Chapter 11 shows how strong GM once was.

GM pioneered one of the unnoticed, but most important, innovations in the auto business – far more important to the health of GM and its competitors than any new engine design or anti-rust coating. GM created the idea of 'this year's model': making a slightly different product each year to encourage us to change our car. This created the new-car-as-status-symbol concept, because people could immediately see whether you had this year's model. GM was slick, compared to fusty, utilitarian old Ford.

But while encouraging owners to change, it encouraged them not to look too far from the source. Ford promised any colour you wanted, as long as it was black. GM wanted you to buy any car you wanted, as long as GM made it.

So this innovation, paradoxically, killed a lot of creativity. While constantly changing models might have been a spur for revolutionary advances in engine or chassis design, or even ways of manufacturing or customer service, instead it encouraged constant fiddly changes while ruling out the fundamental changes that GM needed. This was a decline that showed up in welfare costs and quality problems, but which started, literally, on the drawing board.

Ultimately there were enough people inside GM who believed that every small piece of bad news was just a small problem that could be fixed by a small adjustment, a slight change of strategy, because what it had done had clearly worked.

Hard to make hard choices

Professor Nancy Koehn of Harvard Business School has an idea what the root cause of GM's decline was:

> The three fundamental issues are the management's consistent failure to do the things that made the business so successful initially. First, pay close attention to what's happening in the customers' lives in the context of the larger environment – not only to their stated preferences, but their hopes, dreams, wallets, lifestyles, and values. Second, keep an equally close eye on the competition. And third, understand how a company's structure and culture relate to its strategy. Use all this understanding to place innovative bets.[83]

That's what GM did, she adds, in its early history. It made the company great: the world's largest industrial enterprise for 50 years. As her colleague, associate professor Robert Austin – an auto industry veteran himself – adds, 'When we ran up against the really tough problems, when we started to feel the real pain associated with real change, we pulled back. We were so profitable then, it was hard to muster the will to make the hard choices.'

The hard choices have now been made: since being bailed out by the US government, GM is cutting brands like Pontiac and Hummer, and has even managed to bring an electric car, the Volt, to market, at least 10 years late. It's not that no one knew this was going to happen: over the years there were hundreds of warnings, not least from a market share graph that had dipped to 19 per cent. But GM, staffed (and led) by people who had been inside the organization for a lifetime, had convinced themselves that they were right, and the public were somehow not getting the point. Toyota probably didn't need to try as hard as it did.

For the company who created much of modern management theory, it is 'a failure of leadership as astounding and momentous (and ironic) as the company's early achievement', in the words of Prof. Koehn.

The smell of dead animals *Albania*

Some of the failures in the book ruined little more than a perfectly good idea. It's the nature of modern bankruptcy laws like Chapter 11 in the United States, and administrative receivership in the UK, that a failure can be contained and managed, and the knock-on effects can be minimized. If we're one of the knock-ons, we should be thankful. When a website disappears or we call a number to find the phone is disconnected, we can at least say 'at least nobody died'.

Not so in Albania. It's the most extreme example of the cult of the pyramid scheme in history.[84] In the 1990s, as former communist states emerged from decades of stagnation and discovered the thrill of speculation, some fared better than others. No country fared worse than Albania where, as a result of the boom and bust of its pyramid schemes, the population brought itself to the brink of civil war. Buildings were burnt. At least 2,000 people died.

What seemed to be lifting millions of citizens out of poverty turned out to be a massive money-laundering business that cost lives and livelihoods. This wasn't any old pyramid scheme: at its height about two-thirds of the population had invested in one or other of the many opportunities available to be defrauded. The unpaid liabilities amounted to half the nation's GDP. For a normal country, half the GDP is almost everything that's not spent by the government.

Or, to put it another way, for a couple of years most Albanians spent absolutely everything they had to spare on a crackpot investment scam that was guaranteed to collapse. They wanted to get richer, just like their ex-communist neighbours.

Poorest in Europe

While the social effects of the collapse of communism have been mixed, overall there has been a minor economic miracle. In the mid-1990s, Poland's economy was growing at 7 per cent, Hungary and the Czech Republic at 5 per cent. Further north, Latvia, Lithuania and Estonia were benefitting from trade with Nordic countries, and had begun to create the growth spurt known as the 'Baltic Tiger'. But Albania's backward economy had shrunk by 30 per cent in 1991. Even growing rapidly afterwards, the country was still worse off than it had been under communism.

Albania was, in 1991, the poorest country in Europe. Virtually isolated after the Second World War, the political and financial systems were backward. As in all communist states, there was an underground economy and a small group of private entrepreneurs involved in everything from luxury goods to drug-running. When Albania opened up to a market economy, it had three state banks, almost no private banking, and almost no credit available for citizens who wanted to share in the growing prosperity of central Europe.

An informal network of companies that would take deposits and make loans, created by those entrepreneurs, quickly grew up – and was initially successful at filling the gap. There was no regulation, but the state banks were swamped with bad debt, and so the government actively supported the lenders. Some Albanians were travelling to other countries – banned until the collapse of communism – and sending home money and stories of the market economy. The loans that these companies gave out were the nearest thing that Albania had to a market economy.

However, Albania attempted unregulated growth, because it had no model of bank regulation – and no one who wanted to create one. Weak politicians gave the lenders their support, and the lenders gave the politicians money for their campaigns.

A pyramid scheme is different from a Ponzi scheme. Bernard Madoff took deposits and paid existing investors solely from new deposits. A pyramid scheme often has a legitimate business in there somewhere, but its function is quickly swamped by the need to recruit more investors to pay the returns that the initial investors have been promised. The two models might start in a different place, but they both reach the same destination – because both attract investors by offering unsustainable rates of return. Albania's pyramid schemes offered spectacular rates of interest to finance whatever it was that they were doing.

Some schemes were run by large (by Albanian terms) investors. Some had links to criminal gangs that had profited from smuggling, in violation of United Nations (UN) sanctions during the Balkan war, using the skills learnt under Communism to provide an illegal yet profitable service. The government, delighted that it didn't have to worry about kick-starting the economy, wasn't asking too many questions.

By 1996, word was spreading to an unsophisticated rural population that this is how you could escape from the miserable poverty of life in Europe's forgotten backyard: deposit everything you have in one of these schemes. To them, this was their first taste of what they thought was capitalism. It needed a push to get started – and that push had inadvertently already been given by the UN.

When the UN lifted sanctions against the Federal Republic of Yugoslavia in late 1995, this was generally considered a good thing; the process of normalization in the Balkans was starting. Next door in Albania there were companies for whom smuggling had been a ready source of cash. They needed liquidity to finance extortion and drug-dealing, and so they did this by promising higher returns. The investment schemes bumped up interest rates on their deposits to about 6 or even 8 per cent per month. When one went high, the next went higher. It might have suggested to an experienced investor, who could look at the almost non-existent legitimate businesses at the core of these schemes, that the companies involved weren't planning on giving the money back. But Albania didn't have any experienced investors. Instead it had people who realized they could, apparently, double their money in one year.

For example, the largest scheme was created by an ex-army officer called Vehbi Alimucaj, whose VEFA investment scheme grew out of his business, which was selling soap.[85] By 1993, he already had an annual profit of $639,000. That is, you might think, a lot of soap.

In early 1996, two new schemes – Xhafferi and Populli – came to market. They attracted 2 million investors, more than half the population, in months. Existing schemes raised rates to compete, and a war to attract investment resulted. By September, Populli was offering 30 per cent interest per month. Two months later, Xhafferi was offering to treble your money in two months. Sude offered to double it in two, for those who couldn't wait that long.

In towns Albanians sold houses, in the country they sold cattle. The World Bank reports that Albania literally smelled like a slaughterhouse – why keep cattle in a field when you can double your money by killing them now?

Albania's population assumed that the schemes must be on the level. For 50 years the government ran just about everything in the nominal interests of the workers, so it would protect them from any disaster. Albanians simply fitted the pyramid schemes into their mental picture of the world.

The IMF and the World Bank predicted disaster. The Albanian government loudly disagreed with them and, in post-communist fashion, urged its workers to fill their boots.

Clinging on

On 19 November 1997, Sude became the first scheme to collapse, when it defaulted on its debt. The others quickly lowered rates again, but by January two more had defaulted. At this point the government decided that maybe it should take action, freezing assets and limiting withdrawals to prevent the other schemes emptying their accounts. It was far too late: in short order, faced with the ruin of a large number of its citizens, the government collapsed. Bankrupt police officers deserted and Albanians got angry. A million weapons went missing. Other governments evacuated foreigners quickly.

In Albania, the pyramid schemes were, to the surprise of the population, not too big to fail.

The remaining schemes held on until July, pretending to be solvent in an attempt to get their assets back from the government, some of them laundering their drug money or shipping their remaining cash out of the country. In 1997 output fell by 7 per cent, and inflation rose to 40 per cent.

Christopher Jarvis, who witnessed the problem at first hand for the IMF, points out that the Albanian collapse was avoidable. 'There are steps governments can take to make the growth of pyramid schemes less likely', he wrote in 2000; 'these include establishing a well-functioning financial system, setting up a regulatory framework that covers informal as well as formal markets and has clear lines of responsibility... and tackling general governance problems.'

His final warning, eight years before some much larger investment opportunities were exposed as pyramid schemes: 'the IMF and World Bank should be aware of the possibilities of pyramid schemes emerging when the conditions for growth are present and should be vigilant in warning governments. When they can, the IMF and the World Bank should insist on action.'

But when outsiders warn tight-knit groups of people that they're doing the wrong thing, the group tends not to listen to the outsider. It listens to its leaders, especially if those leaders are promising previously unthinkable wealth.

Alimucaj's VEFA investment scheme claimed to have been investing its depositors' cash in 'business activities'. They were obviously slow to get off the ground: when the fund collapsed in 2007 it had debts of $458 million and business revenues of $2.12 million. VEFA had apparently spent half a billion dollars of seed capital. In reality, Alimucaj used helicopters to fly packets of money out of the country to Italy and Greece. He was later sentenced to five years in prison – served under house arrest in his comfortable villa, with time off for good behaviour. The government – and so the ordinary Albanians – never got their money back. If that happened to you, you'd burn a few buildings down.

MRDA

Herd behaviour is a fact of life: we follow the leader, and failing that, we follow other people who look like they are following a leader, but who might just be following us. When we have a sudden passion or a panic for an investment, a stock or an idea, our herd mentality magnifies the effect.

When we are all buying into something, the price goes up, and validates the idea we're doing the right thing. When everyone agrees that we're making terrific decisions, you get patted on the back when you have an idea that agrees with the consensus.

The consensus has to come from somewhere. In business there is a layer of people whose job it is to help us decide what to think, to provide a feeling of calm in an unpredictable world, to do the hard thinking that we don't have the time or knowledge to do. We need someone to help pick the winners and losers.

They are the analysts.

We rely on analysts to know more than we do, to have greater insight than we do, and to anticipate rather than to react. Most of all, we expect them to be independent. Because if they fail these tests, we might as well play stone, paper, scissors to decide who the winners and losers are.

Most important: independence. On the internet, there's a dismissive phrase: MRDA, or 'Mandy Rice-Davies applies'. It dates to the 1960s, when an alleged prostitute was in court, defending her conduct in a scandal that pulled in a British cabinet minister. When he denied her story, her reply was that 'He would say that, wouldn't he.'[86]

Mandy Rice-Davies might well apply, in subtle and not-so-subtle ways, to the analyst community. Two examples are especially relevant: sell-side analysts and ratings agencies.

Sell-side analysts work for investment banks to produce reports on the companies they follow. Usually they specialize in an industry (for them the AOL–Time Warner merger was a problem. Do we get the internet analyst involved, or the entertainment guys?). They publish their opinion of the companies or sectors they follow, research their strategies, talk to the management on conference calls, look at pages of dull PowerPoint pie charts. They recommend we buy stock in the successes, hold the stock for companies that are treading water, or – for a real car crash – sell. Every company does its best to avoid a 'sell' rating from the analyst: not least because, when the entire management team of a company earns a third or more of its pay in stock, earning a sell rating hits them in the bank account.

And so large, successful companies have a dedicated team to keep analysts feeling positive about them. They have, in industry parlance, an analyst strategy.

The strategy often results in a clear conflict of interest, a conflict which has repeatedly undermined the integrity of their ratings. The conflict is always there, waiting to be exploited. An investment bank earns money from doing business with the companies it rates. Companies do business with investment banks whose analysts rate them highly. A 'sell' rating might be honest, but it also might cost your employer millions of dollars in fees.

As Peter Siris, the CEO of Guerilla Capital Management, put it: 'corporations don't want to do investment banking with somebody who says you're an idiot'.[87]

The linkage might be cynical (I'll reward you for a good rating) or it might be innocent (they obviously understand how extraordinary and talented we are), but a 'buy' rating for a client is good for your colleagues, and probably good for your career as a result. Banks claim a Chinese wall between the analysts and the salespeople, but you'd be either an idiot or brave if you didn't pick up the signals.

Manufacturing consent

The way in which analysts had been captured by their clients became obvious after the collapse of the dot-com boom, when many investment banks were faced with class-action lawsuits and investigations, and after which regulations on their behaviour were tightened. Two analysts in particular were singled out by a Securities and Exchange Commission (SEC) investigation: Jack Grubman of Salomon Smith Barney and Henry Blodget of Merrill Lynch. Both were widely followed superstars, emerging from the shadows to become informal market-makers: their good opinions of these strange internet companies meant that people bought the stock, because no one, ultimately, understood what the dot-commers did, or how they would make money.

Both were banned from the industry for life after the SEC investigated how they arrived at those ratings. Analysts, they discovered, owned shares in the companies that they recommended – which had often been bought at discount prices. Firms did not track the investment decisions of their analysts. At Merrill Lynch, an investigation into Blodget's team showed analysts privately referring to stock that they had recommended as 'a piece of junk', and in one case, that one of their recommendations had nothing to recommend it 'except the banking fees'.

Ten firms – every major investment bank on Wall Street – settled with the SEC, paying $1.4 billion to settle the investigation. The chairman of the SEC called it a 'sad chapter in the history of American business'.[88]

At Merrill Lynch, analyst Jonathan Cohen gave Amazon.com a 'sell' rating in 1998. The stock was overvalued, he reasoned (a 'sell' doesn't have to mean the company is failing, just that it isn't worth its stock price. If we apply that logic rigorously, then either the efficient markets hypothesis applies, in which case everything would be rated neutral; or it doesn't, in which case there would be as many 'sells' as 'buys'). A woman who worked in Merrill's printing office called to ask if he'd made a mistake – she'd never seen a report with the pink cover that is reserved for a 'sell' recommendation.

It wasn't just dot-com entrepreneurs who knew how to manufacture consent. If there is a case study in how to manipulate analyst opinion it is, not surprisingly, provided by Enron.

It was an open secret that a good rating meant that Enron rewarded your bank, and the process was monitored internally by Enron management. In 2000 Enron paid $250m in fees to banks. Six earned more than $20 million: Merrill Lynch, Credit Suisse First Boston, Donaldson Lufkin & Jenrette, Citigroup, Chase and JP Morgan.

A *Financial Times* article from 2002 reported that 'Enron kept track of how much it paid each bank, and was careful to spread the work around, especially its underwriting assignments'. It worked: in September 2001, when Enron was already vulnerable, 16 analysts gave the stock a 'buy' rating and only one rated it 'hold'.[89]

John Olson covered Enron for Merrill Lynch and later Sanders Morris Harris. He perceived that Enron saw analysts as either for it or against it. 'In one telephone call… the then CEO told me quite succinctly, "We are for our friends," and proceeded to itemize the monthly history of my own "unfriendly" Enron ratings over the prior two years.'

The one holdout from the 'buy' consensus paid for his independence: on August 23 2001, Daniel Scotto of BNP Paribas SA, a 30-year veteran, gave Enron a 'neutral' rating, downgrading it from 'buy'. He told investors that

Enron was highly leveraged and lacked hard assets; stock 'should be sold at all costs and sold now', he said. He didn't actually rate Enron as a 'sell', claiming afterwards he would have been 'guillotined' if he had (Scotto is French by birth).

BNP placed Scotto on a 12-week leave, then fired him. Scotto claimed the two events were related, though BNP denied any link.

Reason to believe

There is, also, a more innocent (though no less damaging) explanation why ratings on successful companies often don't become negative until it's too late for the investors who are following the recommendation. Having spent so much time with these companies, having heard all the good stories which dominate their discussions, the media, their conversations in bars after work, and having been congratulated over their intelligence in spotting a star early and making the 'buy' call that earned the trading desk a lot of money, analysts are unintentionally blind to problems. They see the best in the companies they follow.

Enron again: as the company was collapsing, it held a conference call on 23 October 2001. Analysts, who had rated Enron a 'buy' for the previous 12 months while the stock had lost three-quarters of its value, listened to what Lehman Brothers analyst Richard Gross called 'an inadequate defense of the balance sheet'. He rated the stock 'strong buy', saying that 'the stock should recover sharply'.[90]

When the Senate Governmental Affairs Committee asked Gross to justify this rating in February 2002, Gross relied: 'The basic business model we believed was very strong, was growing rapidly, was portable into other commodities and that this was the strength of Enron.' We know now that he had more faith in Enron at that point than Enron had in itself.

John Coffee, a professor at Columbia Law School and a member of advisory committees to the SEC and the National Association of Securities Dealers, points out that most analysts are honest, and their advice has – overall – been better than neutral. He also points out that there are more 'buys' than 'sells' because no one is interested in failing businesses: 'Analysts tend to follow the stocks they like. There is a selection bias. So that to say they follow stocks that they like it's because they pick the ones they like. They don't follow the ones that they consider to be losers', he explains.

The problem is that when you approach a company because you're a fan of it, you might not be a reliable analyst of it afterwards.

Cheerleaders

After MRDA, another set of initials: NRSRO, or Nationally Recognized Statistical Rating Organization. Who are these people? you ask. We know them better by their names: Moody's, Standard & Poors, Fitch. The three companies rate risk, and are given NRSRO status by the US SEC as the three reliable arbiters of investments and the creditworthiness of their issuers, even when those issuers are governments. When we hear that mortgage-backed securities were AAA rated, it was these three companies that rated them that way. When the news reports that Greece or Russia's credit rating was downgraded, one of these companies did it.

Although recently they have begun to explain how and why they come up with their ratings, we're never going to know exactly how they do it: if we did, then we could all come up with the ratings for ourselves, and so we wouldn't need them anymore. To stay in business their rating methods have to be opaque. They are three black boxes.

Trusting the black box is one of the problems that caused the 2007 crisis: mortgage-backed securities (themselves something of a black box) rated as the risk-free highest grade AAA investments turned out to be fizzing bombs instead. The rating underestimated the effect of homeowners defaulting, but also effectively ruled out the scenario that, if they did, that risk would have an impact of the banks' balance sheets. The AAA rating skewed risk management in every bank, pension and hedge fund that relied on the rating, because everyone was exposed to mortgage-backed securities.

That's just the wrong call. By itself, it doesn't mean there's a systemic problem. But the power of the NRSROs is such that, if you want to issue any kind of debt, the price you need to pay to borrow money is largely determined by the rating you get. Whereas for most of their existence the agencies have been an aid to pricing risk, now they effectively decide the price. We have a cognitive bias – a gut reaction – to believe that the value of something is the first price we hear for it. The first price we hear for risk is governed by the NRSROs.

There's good news: these three companies avoid the conflicts of interest to which the sell-side analysts are exposed. On the other hand, this is replaced by a different problem: companies pay to be rated (someone has to pay, after all). They are expecting something for their money. When the company gets a bad rating, analysts are exposed to an all-out attack to show them they were wrong. There's no one to argue for the other side. It's like having a trial with no case for the defence. If you were drawing up a ratings process in a perfect world, this isn't the one you would create.

There's a final problem: because agencies have a natural tendency to stick to their ratings, the evidence from the credit crisis is that they often downgrade late and dramatically. They are intended to provide market stability, but a sudden change in the rating does the opposite. In 2007, $1.9 trillion in mortgage-backed securities were suddenly downgraded from risk-free to various degrees of riskiness. The rating was appropriate: just far too late. Even if banks didn't want to dump the securities as a result, they had to: suddenly they owned too many assets that were classified as risky. The resulting fire-sale of collateralized debt obligations (CDOs) made the credit crisis much worse.[91]

Can this be fixed? The problem is that, as a recent paper in the *University of Miami Law Review* points out, the underestimation of risk for this type of security during the housing bubble was economically rational.[92] Because rating those products became such a large proportion of the agencies' business, and because their liability for an inaccurate rating was limited (or so they thought: several large investors are suing the agencies), the benefits of over-rating were greater than the cost.

When it comes to the systemic, though accidental, creation of bubbles, it's not just optimism that's the problem. We may be getting bad advice.

Chapter Six
Greater fools

> *It's not the despair... It's the hope I can't stand.* JOHN CLEESE

The greater fool theory of investing means that you don't have to believe that what you're buying is worth what you pay for it, as long as there's someone else who is prepared to buy it from you for more than you paid.

That's the nature of an economic bubble. Plenty of research demonstrates that we're rarely aware of when we're in a bubble, and unable to predict when we've encountered the greatest fool, and the bubble is about to burst. All sudden failures in this book have a bit of the bubble about them – a sense afterwards that we were gripped by a collective madness, a financial hangover.

While the Tulip Mania (p 122) shows us that bubbles don't need technology, electronic markets, complex financial instruments, or shareholder economies to exist, the examples of bubbles in this section show how a collective madness can grow from a perfectly normal reaction: that people who have little to lose and much to gain from speculation, when handed an opportunity that they don't fully grasp, will naturally go for it. When we look back and laugh at them, we're ignoring the fact that we do the same. We like to buy houses when the prices are going up, even though economic theories say that there should be less demand when prices rise. We tell ourselves that you never lose money on a house, when even the experience of the past 20 years shows us that, often, we do lose money.

The news media celebrates risk-takers who succeed as modern gods. It admires winners and ignores losers. The speculator's game of choice for 100 years was contract bridge, in which you cooperate with your partner to make a contract based on the value of the assets – cards – you have, then carefully marshal your resources to achieve your goal. Today's CEOs prefer poker. It's a game of considerable skill but based on aggression, maximizing your personal resources at the expense of others. In poker you can win with poor cards, as long as there's a bigger fool than you at the table.

Fund manager Howard Marks, the founder of Oaktree Capital, talks about 'The seven worst words in the world: too much money chasing too few deals. When that happens, run for the hills.' This is what happened to the people who didn't follow that advice.

Feeding risk *Lehman Brothers*

In 2005, Raghuram G Rajan, then chief economist of the International Monetary Fund (IMF) and now a professor at the University of Chicago Booth School of Business, presented a controversial paper at the annual Jackson Hole monetary conference. The title: 'Has Financial Development Made the World Riskier?'[93] The question wasn't controversial. The answer, though, was: yes.

At the time, the financial instruments that banks such as Lehman Brothers had created were widely credited with removing risk from banking, while boosting returns. It seemed ridiculous that in the middle of a long boom, with few predictions that it would end, Rajan should issue a warning that it all might suddenly end. Bank employees, he said, had incentives to take risks that were concealed from investors, because then they looked as if they were achieving better returns than their peers: 'Typically, the kinds of risks that can be concealed most easily, given the requirement of periodic reporting, are risks that generate severe adverse consequences with small probability but, in return, offer generous compensation the rest of the time', he said.

To do this, banks required liquidity: to buy and sell risk, and to borrow large amounts to fund their investments. It meant, Rajan warned, that it was also much tougher to work out when a bank was in danger simply by looking at its assets:

> As plain-vanilla risks can be moved off bank balance sheets into the balance sheets of investment managers, banks have an incentive to originate more of them. Thus, they will tend to feed rather than restrain the appetite for risk. However, banks cannot sell all risks. They often have to bear the most complicated and volatile portion of the risks they originate... Their greater reliance on market liquidity can make their balance sheets more suspect in times of crisis.

Three years later, on the evening of 12 September 2008, US Treasury Secretary Hank Paulson called the chief executive officers (CEOs) of America's global banking community together for an emergency meeting. Lehman Brothers, one of the oldest, largest and most successful of their number, was not going to open for business on Monday, he told them, unless they could find a way to save it. There was to be no government bail out for Lehman.

As the banking establishment debated, phoned, met and e-mailed over the weekend, it soon became clear that there was to be no private sector bail out either. As they looked at Lehman's books, the CEOs of its competitors discovered that to save the bank would take a cash injection of between $20 billion and $25 billion. At that point in the financial crisis, no one was going to put up that kind of money.

The firing line

Well, almost no one. Barclays Bank, based in London, sent the message that it would be prepared to buy Lehman's business.[94] The Bank of England and the Financial Services Authority, far from applauding an audacious financial rescue, were horrified. 'I thought there was a real risk that if it tried to swallow this thing whole, [Barclays] would put itself in the firing line', said Sir John Gieve, at that time deputy governor of the Bank of England.

Lehmans' trouble was so deep, its predicament so horrible, that no other bank could save it – because Lehman might drag that bank down too.

Almost everyone and anything connected with banking or mortgages has been apportioned its share of blame for bringing the 160-year story of Lehman Brothers to an abrupt close in September 2008. Memoirs have dug deep into the counterfactuals: what might have happened if banks had not invested so much in sub-prime mortgages, if the derivatives of those mortgages hadn't been given an AAA credit rating, if Barclays Bank hadn't been blocked from saving Lehman, if the US Treasury Secretary hadn't been so intransigent, if CEO Richard Fuld had acted earlier or been able to see that failure was possible.

Dominating all those narratives: what would have happened if Lehman had not been leveraged at more than 30:1?

To explain the jargon: the sort of financial trades which Lehman was using to generate its profits (and which its competitors used too) needed huge amounts of borrowed money. This isn't money that sits in a vault, or even can be clearly identified as belonging to one institution. It is enough to know it was there, backing a deal. Being leveraged at 30:1 means that to make a deal, Lehman equity was combined with 30 times as much borrowed money to buy the financial products it bought. Just as when you buy a house with a mortgage, you pay more money back, but as long as the asset you buy makes a bigger return than the cost of leverage, you don't mind. Compared to the profit you can make from just investing your equity, the rewards are huge.

All the major merchant banks were leveraged at close to this level – Goldman Sachs slightly less, others slightly more. Most are still at this level today. It's actually impossible to know for sure, because one response to the crisis has been for banks to become more adept at moving their risky assets 'off balance sheet', to avoid frightening investors. Also, you can be leveraged at any level you like, as long as the risk you take is appropriate to the level of borrowing.

Former Lehman vice president (VP) Larry McDonald – the author of *A Colossal Failure of Common Sense* about his time at the company – points out that in 1998 the balance sheet of Lehman was worth $38 billion. By 2007, it was worth $780 billion. Its assets were equivalent to one-third of the output of the UK economy.

Lehman tripped up because it was seen as the most vulnerable of the investment banks to a shift in the market – a shift that could have destroyed any one of them. When the markets decided that Lehman's risk and Lehman's leverage didn't match up, they acted quickly.

Who next?

Many of the stories of sudden failure imply a catastrophe of sorts: a fraud uncovered, a sudden panic, a run on the bank. When you are leveraged at 30:1, the odds of a bank-ending event are substantially shorter, because if the value of the assets you hold drops by 3 per cent, and your investors want to sell out, you're insolvent. Your equity base does not cover the losses.

That's a simple fact of capitalism. It was natural to let Lehman fail, because it had done what we all do once in our lives, and borrowed an amount that it couldn't pay back. This was becoming obvious by the Sunday afternoon, when the banking community accepted that Lehman could not be saved. In New York, London and offices worldwide, taxis arrived at Lehman headquarters and employees removed their belongings in cardboard boxes, in case the offices were closed on Monday. The spectacle was performed in front of the global press, which further panicked the remaining banks. If this could happen to Lehman, who was next?

In truth, no one was next. Merrill Lynch was the next domino that looked set to fall, but CEO John Thain saw the way the negotiations were heading on the weekend of 12 September, stepped out of the meeting, and sold his bank to Bank of America. 'Allowing Lehman to fail was a huge mistake', he says now, because the problem for everyone that was left was that their leveraged positions would take years to unwind – but they had only hours to live if they couldn't convince investors that they were solvent. Suddenly, for all the banks, it was all-or-nothing.

Rajan's nightmare scenario had arrived. Liquidity had dried up. No one wanted to do business with anyone else, because no one knew whether it was a good or bad idea to do so. The Bank of International Settlements values the market in derivatives for the year ending 2009 at $1,200 trillion. Derivatives were famously described by Warren Buffet as 'financial weapons of mass destruction'. There were a lot of fizzing bombs around, but no one knew which of the banks was holding the bombs that were about to go off.

The abyss

'We were as close as I've ever seen it to the edge of the abyss' is how Rodgin Cohen, a partner at law firm Sullivan and Cromwell, and an advisor to Lehman, remembers that time.

And yet no one else fell into the abyss at that moment. That's because the next into the pit was AIG, a company which had gambled everything on supporting the massive leveraged positions that Lehman and others had adopted. The government had let Lehman go, but it bailed out AIG. And around the world, Lehman's bankruptcy sparked global action that involved governments in $15 trillion of bail outs. That's about 25 per cent of global GDP. Lehman's leverage, and the huge amount of financial products it bought using it, had created a problem that took the equivalent of $2,000 from everyone on the planet to sort out.

When we borrow money and get into debt, we usually resolve to live within our means for a while: the bank stops us borrowing so much money until we learn how to manage it. At the time of writing, banks worldwide aren't keen to take their own medicine. They are still discussing what their 'means' – fixed by suitable leverage caps – might be. Governments could tell them, but they became subservient to the banking industry long ago. No country wants to frighten off its tax-paying financial sector by imposing a lower cap than its neighbour, even if it means that we reflate the bubble.

The US government intended to impose a maximum leverage ratio of 15:1 in its banking reforms of 2010, which would have severely curtailed the amount of risk that investment banks could take with other people's money. However, by the time the bill became law, the new Financial Stability Oversight Council could impose the 15:1 debt-to-equity limit on a firm only if it poses a 'grave threat' to system-wide financial stability: it's now a sanction, not a rule, and one that is, in reality, easy to avoid in the now-you-see-it-now-you-don't world of leverage. Until it was too late, no one considered the behaviour of

Lehman Brothers or its competitors any kind of 'threat' at all – except a few economists like Rajan.

Lehman Brothers is history, but banks continue to attempt to outdo each other by making bigger leveraged bets, and moving more assets off balance sheet. The actual levels of leverage are anyone's guess. Now the bubble is reflated, the banks use their terrifying leverage to make fabulous profits, some of which they give back to the government who lent them the money to stay in business after the last bubble popped. This is the world we made.

Strengthened by government money, and higher profits in an investment market with less competition, banks are lobbying fiercely against restraint of their leverage. In the United States, as the economist Joseph Stiglitz points out, there are five times as many banking industry lobbyists as there are members of Congress. 'They had the incentive to be short sighted, to take excessive risk', he says. 'If you gamble and win, you walk off with the profits. If you gamble and lose, the government bails you out. So why not gamble?'

Confidence at its height *The Tulip Mania*

Lehman Brothers's collapse wasn't the first time that supposedly financially prudent people went, to use a technical term, bonkers. When William Shakespeare had Cassius say that 'The fault, dear Brutus, is not in our stars, But in ourselves', the first roots of an odd financial disaster had just been planted – literally. The Tulip Mania of 1636 is the oldest of the failures in this book. It may also be the silliest. But not by much. As best as historians can divine, it's a disaster that shows how, when the stars align correctly, there isn't much wisdom in crowds.[95]

The Tulip Mania, in which – for a few months – the prices of tulip bulbs rocketed, is an interesting historical curiosity, but it's far more than that. We still don't know all the details of how much money changed hands and who the winners and losers were, but that's just like a modern financial crisis. We are not 100 per cent sure what made people indulge in such reckless financial speculation – and whether, even, the Tulip Mania was the financial disaster we thought it was. So, in short, it's like every other stock market crisis in the four centuries that followed.

The Tulip Mania is the first great bubble in the modern era, and it involved Dutch merchants paying spectacular prices for tulip bulbs, and selling them on for even more ridiculous amounts. The popular account that made the story well known was recorded by Charles Mackay, in his *Extraordinary Popular Delusions*, published in 1841. As a journalist and a contemporary and acquaintance of Charles Dickens, Mackay loved a good story, and he tells the tale of the fashion for purchasing rare tulip bulbs among the Dutch merchant classes with relish, even if we can't rely completely on his sources.

'Until the year 1634 the tulip annually increased in reputation, until it was deemed a proof of bad taste in any man of fortune not to be without a collection of them', he tells us. That is unwise, and unexpected for a nation of merchants as skilled and level-headed as the Dutch, but every society occasionally develops passions which, even a few months later, are inexplicable. How else are we to explain the success of the Cabbage Patch Doll, or the Jonas Brothers? Nevertheless, the sums in Mackay's account are staggering. One bulb of a variety called Semper Augustus was sold in 1636 for 12 acres of building ground, he tells us, and another for 4,600 florins (about £30,000) plus a carriage, two grey horses and a complete suit of harness. Another root, known as Viceroy, was listed by a contemporary author as having sold for goods to the value of 2,500 florins, including four oxen, a bed, a suit of clothes and 'One thousand lbs. of cheese'.

The Dutch merchants were great financial innovators. At this time Amsterdam had a stock exchange, and it is no surprise that trade in tulips became a large part of the trade on the exchange. 'Confidence was at its height, and everybody gained. The tulip-jobbers speculated in the rise and fall of the tulip stocks, and made large profits... a golden bait hung temptingly out before the people. Everyone imagined that the passion for tulips would last forever', Mackay tells us.

As more of the population was involved in the trade, and the job of 'tulip-notary' became common in Holland's towns, more people entered the market not because they wanted the rarest flowers, but because they wanted the money that came from trading the bulbs out of season. This was, in part, because the trade in bulbs didn't need to be settled immediately, and so by buying and selling the same bulb in a rising market the participants could turn an immediate paper profit, with no need to actually keep bulbs lying around.

A futures market

It was, in effect, one of the first futures markets in existence: you would contract not for the bulb immediately, but for the delivery of the bulb when it was in season. The price explosion occurred between November 1636 and February 1637.

At the peak of tulip mania on 3 February 1637, some single tulip bulbs sold for more than 10 times the annual income of a skilled craftsman.

Finally, as the market inevitably collapsed, Holland counted the cost. In Mackay's description: 'Those who were unlucky enough to have had stores of tulips on hand at the time of the sudden reaction were left to bear their ruin as philosophically as they could; those that had made profits were allowed to keep them.' And yet the Dutch had not lost their love for tulips by 1841, when Mackay wrote that they boasted of them in the same way that an Englishman boasted of fine racehorses or old pictures.

We have some reason to doubt the absolute veracity of Mackay's tale, because he was writing second-hand from contemporary sources who were against this new fashion of speculation, and so they went long on the craziness and short on the explanation. And there are some explanations. One, favoured by the economist Peter Garber, is that the contracts were never meant to be enforced, and that as Holland was ridden with plague, few took the bubble seriously. He calls the Tulip Mania a 'meaningless winter drinking game'.[96]

Others point to the fact that the guild of Dutch florists were lobbying for the futures contracts to be made unenforceable – that you were merely paying a small amount for the right to buy the bulb at that price at a later date.[97] It's what in modern financial parlance is an option (see the story of Long Term Capital Management for what can happen when you trade in options). If the contracts were de facto options, it's not a bubble: the buyers merely declined to take up the options if prices fell.

The evidence: on 24 February 1637, the guild announced that all futures contracts written after 30 November 1636 were option contracts.

Yet these things we know: the Dutch went crazy for tulips, and then quickly became sane again. The price of a bulb fell 99.999 per cent between its peak on 3 February 1637 and 1 May the same year. Whether they were speculating because they thought they might die, or they knew they would never have to pay up, they took one of the first successful stock markets and sent it crazy with speculation.

The long-term effects for the Dutch were significant, because for the first time there was a widespread idea that a simple commodity – a flower that didn't yet exist – could have more value than a person's yearly wage. One of the reasons that we know so much about a relatively short-term bubble was that the Tulip Mania was exaggerated by religious pamphlets as a warning against speculation and putting too much value in earthly things. It's a warning that the believers and unbelievers alike have completely ignored ever since.

The greatest financier *Charles Ponzi*

Charles Ponzi, who must surely qualify as one of the 20th century's great business innovators (but not in a good way), arrived in the United States in 1903 from Parma in Italy with $2.50 in his pocket. It wasn't a good start to his new life. He had set off with $200, but gambled the rest away on the voyage. There's a card-player's maxim that, if you are looking for the fool at the gambling table, and you can't see who it is, it's you.

Ponzi, it turned out, might have been a fraudster, but in public relations terms he was no fool. He knew how to blow a bubble. He had something far more valuable than money: he could convince intelligent people that he was a financial genius.[98]

The crackpot scheme which now bears his name was set up by Ponzi from the office of his import/export company in Boston in 1919. Having worked in casual jobs all over the United States and Canada, he was married, and wanted to establish his own business: his idea was to set up a magazine called *The Trader's Guide*.

It's a pity for his later investors that it never got off the ground, or he might have ended his days as an obscure Bostonian publisher. When setting up international mailing, though, Ponzi had observed that an International Reply Coupon from another country was worth more in the United States than it was in the country of origin.

That, he decided, was his chance to be rich. He would buy coupons overseas and sell them in the United States for a profit.

He set up the Securities and Exchange Company to manage this business, but his real genius was in obtaining finance from the general public, rather than from sceptical banks. He offered promissory notes to investors who could contribute as little as $10, saying that he would pay them back in 90 days with 50 per cent interest on top. He cleverly paid his original investors back in 45 days, implying that the business exceeded even his expectations. At the beginning of 1920, 18 people had invested in his scheme to redeem International Reply Coupons. Six months later, 30,219 people held promissory notes, an investment at that time of $15 million, or $165 million in 2010. That was for a business that was little more than six months old, and had not received any press coverage or done any advertising.

Ponzi was a hero of the people: as an immigrant and self-made man, he was celebrated by the working classes. As a man who paid 50 per cent interest in 45 days, he was lauded by the rich. They all queued side-by-side on the steps of his offices to redeem their notes and reinvest their money.

In the words of William McNary, the treasurer of the Hanover Trust Company and a former congressman, Ponzi was 'the greatest financier America has ever produced'. Experts went on record to say that the scheme was financially sound. No one stopped to check whether he was actually selling any reply coupons using the money that had been invested.

Doing good

Ponzi schemes – named after the model popularized by the man, rather than invented by him – usually claim to have some incredible insight into the investment process that makes such profits possible, and claim to be paying the dividends out of abundant profits. They rely on greater fools, but early investors don't look foolish at all. More people invest, the scheme grows rapidly, few of us care whether or not the business is sound in the long term – all our mates are making out, so we want a piece of the action.

In 1920, five-foot-two Ponzi would arrive for work in a limousine, with crowds cheering. The police would hold back the crowds who jammed the streets. Inside his office the clerks had no time for bookkeeping. They simply stuffed the money into drawers in their desks.

When a minor scandal broke in July, and Ponzi was being sued by another businessman who claimed that Ponzi owed him $1 million, the entrepreneur was never slow to come forward and announce that he had 30 times that amount in the bank. He had a peculiar talent to inspire: by pretending that he didn't need the money, he attracted even more of it. Ponzi carried a cheque for $1 million in his top pocket, and promised to 'do good in the world' with the rest of his profits when he retired.

You might have thought that press stories like the unpaid millionaire would dampen speculation in Ponzi's scheme, yet the pattern that we were to see almost 100 years later in the case of Bernard Madoff was established: the authorities, given clear evidence that there was no possibility that the scheme was real (which, a few months later, everyone would agree was clearly the case), reached precisely the opposite conclusion. Despite the Boston police and the state attorney general investigating this business, investors still blocked the street outside his office. Eventually, two of the three police officers who were sent to investigate invested instead.

Two things occurred: on the outside, small investors often got in over their heads. The second is that a small business quickly becomes a monster that constantly needs profits to pay out. If there were $15 million of notes in circulation on 1 July 1920, that meant that in the next 50 days Ponzi would have to lay his hands on $7.5 million in cash simply to keep those investors happy. The only way to do that in the short term is to sell more notes.

Doing bad

Eventually, you are taking money in the front door and sending it out the back door. As long as the business grows exponentially, you can do this. As soon as it stops taking new investments you have a problem – unless the profits from sales of International Reply Coupons can fill the gap.

The evidence was finally too much to ignore. When *The Boston Post* published a series of critical articles, stating that the business was unsustainable, it pointed out that if Ponzi could make these profits, why would he keep any money in a bank, as he claimed? Ponzi reacted by promising to refund anyone who wasn't convinced. It backfired: hundreds took up the offer.

On 30 July 1920, the New York postmaster did a long-overdue calculation, and pointed out that the world's total supply of International Reply Coupons, if they were all bought and traded by Ponzi, would not support the profits he was paying. The federal government belatedly became interested and started an investigation. The queues outside his office dwindled.

In August, Ponzi's own publicist wrote an article that revealed that Ponzi had never made any investments overseas, that the money would soon run out, and that his business was insolvent. Ponzi reacted by claiming he could pay everyone, and that if anyone wanted to be paid he or she should come to the office.

By 9 August 1920, those who had decided to take their money had done so, but Ponzi was, incredibly, still in business, and investors were still buying the notes. But the game was up. With his bank accounts frozen Ponzi couldn't pay any more dividends. He had liabilities of $7 million and assets of $4 million.

Amazingly, in the face of clear evidence that the business was both impossible and fraudulent, a large number of note holders hung on to their worthless paper. Some went to the grave believing that Ponzi was, as he claimed, the victim of jealous competitors and that he could have paid all his investors; he was often cheered on the street. When the list of creditors was published, some had invested up to £33,000. Three-quarters of the Boston police were investors. Six banks collapsed. Ponzi was convicted of mail fraud in 1920, was later tried and convicted as a 'common and notorious thief' in 1925, and sentenced to seven more years. Afterwards he was deported back to Italy, and finished his life working for a different kind of con artist: Mussolini.

The Securities and Exchange Company's total investment in International Reply Coupons, the apparent source of the fabulous profits, was a few hundred dollars.

Promises, promises *Home-Stake Production Co*

If there's one thing that makes better news copy than a fool, it's a rich fool. 'Getting Penny Pincher Jack Benny to kick $300,000 into a shaky oil scheme is no easy job. Enticing Financial Cognoscente George J.W. Goodman ("Adam Smith," author of *The Money Game*[99]) to chip in $110,000 seemingly should be even harder. Or consider trying to gull $211,000 out of Walter Wriston, chairman of the First National City Bank', *Time Magazine* proposed in July 1974, reporting on how these three celebrities – plus around 2,000 more – had been persuaded to invest in an oil-drilling adventure dreamed up by an Oklahoma lawyer called Robert S Trippet.[100]

Home-Stake Production Co's Ponzi scheme has been dwarfed by others since, and a loss of $130 million, compared to the billions swallowed by Bernard Madoff, seems almost quaint. But it is the purest example of a Ponzi that flourished because we so dearly want to invest alongside successful people. The pull to peer-association was so great that bankers ignored their own company's researchers, and a business prospectus that any experienced investor would have dismissed as a poor joke pulled in the 2010 equivalent of more than half a billion dollars.

The list of creditors, exposed when the scheme filed for bankruptcy, shows that Hollywood stars and bank chief executives flocked to give their money to a company that had no track record, no income and – if they looked closely – little hope of ever giving them back their money.

Trippet, apparently an excellent salesman, sold $130 million of subscriptions for his oil-drilling scheme. He told prospective investors that they would make 300 or 400 per cent returns from drilling for oil in California. Instead, when oil drilling proved more difficult than he expected, Trippet's staff persuaded a farmer to let them paint his irrigation pipes pink and orange and attached codes to them, so that people who visited the site thought that oil was already flowing through them. The money kept flowing in – there just wasn't any oil to sell.

Not about the oil

How could an amateurish fraud like this succeed? There are two reasons. The first is that Trippet was never shy in discreetly letting potential investors know who else had put their money into Home-Stake. He wasn't selling oil – he was selling the opportunity to join a very select club that famous and successful people were part of. That works both for the famous and successful people (who wanted to invest in the same scheme as their peers) and for people who are not famous and successful, who want to get inside the velvet rope.

Word of the get-rich-quick scheme spread as gossip among its A-list investors. Trippet may have been lousy at drilling for oil, but he knew how to work a room. Other investors included Alan Alda ($145,000), Barbra Streisand ($28,500) and Bob Dylan ($78,000). The former chairman of General Electric put up $440,920; the president of American Express, $57,000 and the chairman of PepsiCo an unknown amount.

Maybe we can excuse Barbra Streisand for not knowing much about oil exploration, but the long list of senior bank executives should have been content, in the words of Robert Metzger, then president of investment advisor Resource Programs, to 'sit down and read the Home-Stake prospectus and laugh', as Metzger's specialist advisors did. Instead they invested in this glamorous business – sometimes against the advice of their own research departments.

Trippet also knew how to shore up the illusion of success. Some of his A-list investors were paid excellent dividends – in truth, paid for by the recent or non-famous investors who, thanks to a careful division of dividends, would not see their money back. Western Union Chairman Russell W McFall ($60,000) was paid a dividend of $6,220, and no doubt told his friends and colleagues what an easy source of cash this was.

Trippet, found guilty of criminal charges in December 1976, spent one day in jail, and lost a civil case from those who wanted to reclaim their money – much of which no longer existed.

Always on hand after the event, in 1974 the Securities and Exchange Commission in the United States issued a public warning to investors when the details of Home-Stake were made public. It warned them not to fall for 'get-rich-quick schemes, promising spectacular returns without any basis of fact'. This warning has, to date, been universally ignored.

Boys will be boys

When Michael Lewis quit as a trader at Salomon Brothers to write *Liar's Poker* about his time there as a fabulously paid 'big swinging d*ck' trader in the 1980s, he had an ambition for his book: he wanted to show everyone how pointless it was to do that job.

'I thought what I'd described was a kind of wasted life,' he says now, 'and I'm overwhelmed by letters from college students saying, "I read your book, and I'm even more excited by going to Wall Street than I was before. Do you have any tips you kept out of your book?"' Lewis is still outraged by the conduct of Wall Street, and still thinks we should be too.

On the other hand, there are no words that will prevent large numbers of young (always) men (usually) from becoming even more excited by the idea of trading. So, given that their activity can create and destroy wealth under the noses of their CEOs faster than those CEOs ever could, what are the forces that make them perform well or, in the macho terminology that traders use for just about everything, 'blow up'?

The idea that traders find the correct price comes primarily from the 'efficient markets hypothesis', which is one of the few parts of trading that is simple enough for the outsider to understand. In a freely traded market, everything is at its appropriate price, because all the bad news makes people sell, which reduces the price, and all the good news makes people buy, which increases the price. The fluctuations in a share price, for example, represent random activity, not information – all the information is built into the price already.

This hypothesis breaks down in many situations. Panic is one: the feeling that others know something, so you must sell. Sometimes, in the case of insider dealing, this is true (and not legal). Enthusiasm is another – when a price goes up, as happens with house prices, more of us get involved. Hence bubbles. Over-trading is another: if everything was at the correct price, you'd still have thousands of traders who can't sit still, and so they'd find a justification for buying and selling, and the herd mentality will create a narrative that sends a price tumbling or soaring.[101]

So, for a mechanism that creates efficiency and transparency, trading also has some important faults. And many of those faults stem from the people we employ to do the job, and the situations which have become tradable. The consequences of those faults can destroy a healthy company. Some are captured by the idea that trading is controllable and always healthy. Others simply don't have the slightest idea that their traders are eating the company from under them, like thousands of adrenaline-fuelled financial termites.

Off-peak performance

Doug Hirschhorn, a 'Peak Performance Coach' for top traders, asks his students whether, if there is a game that they would win 95 per cent of the time, they would play it. Most immediately say 'yes', because traders love to gamble, and this is as close to a sure thing as they will ever see. This is a dangerous answer if you're giving those traders your money.

Hirschhorn, who has worked with many of the major investment banks, including Credit Suisse, is surprisingly negative about those whose peak performance he is developing. The problem is, he says, that when traders make money, no one cares very much how they do it.

'A lot of people look the other way. People don't care about fixing things when it's working, they care about how they are going to get paid', he says. 'For example, only 10 per cent of my clients go to the expense of having the personality of traders screened before they employ them.'

With the ability to trade comes a set of personality traits which, when the environment changes, can be destructive to the company.

The first is that traders are rarely deeply analytical. They prefer to live in the moment, and see the win rather than the consequences of losing. They win most of the time, but when they lose, they lose big. This is what's known in the business as 'blowing up'. There's a school of thought that if a trader blows up early, it's a valuable lesson.

This is the purpose of Hirschhorn's 95 per cent winning game. Imagine that each time you win the prize is £5, but when you lose the loss is £100. Your expected winnings would be $19 \times 5 - 100$, which means you expect to lose £5 every time you play 20 games. So the smart traders ask, what might I lose?

'They tend to have a gambling mentality. They just look at the problems, not at the probabilities and the outcomes, and under pressure they fall back into that ingrained personality', explains Hirschhorn. 'They get paid an obscene amount of money. They are not curing cancer, or finding new ways to feed people. It draws the sort of person who is attracted to that sensation-seeking behaviour.'

The second problem is that traders trade. They don't do anything else. They are scared of missing out, and so they act, even when there's nothing good they can achieve. When Jerome Kerveil lost €6 billion for Société Générale, he took small losses and doubled down. The collapse of Barings Bank followed the same pattern. Alpesh Patel, author of *The Mind of a Trader*, says that 'if you can remove yourself from wanting to make money, then ironically that's more likely to get you the money. If most traders would learn how to sit on their hands 50 per cent of the time, they would make a lot more money.'[102]

This means that the most likely way in which a trader will try to get out of a problem is devising a new way to trade out of it. In an extreme situation, this can be disastrous. When Bear Stearns was losing billions on toxic sub-prime mortgages, the trader responsible, Ralph Cioffi, created a second fund. The first was leveraged 35 times, the second was leveraged 100 times. When that blew up, he created a company called Everquest Financial and planned an initial public offering (IPO) for it, whose main asset was the 'toxic waste' that was sinking his funds.

When management eventually realized what he was doing, it stopped the flotation, but the damage had been done.

What are you doing?

Which brings us to the third problem. Traders are pragmatic: they do what they can get away with. Imposing rules on traders might solve some problems, but it creates a puzzle for them to solve, because a strict set of rules is basically a road map of exactly the behaviour to avoid. Anything else: go ahead.

'A lot of behaviour is driven by how many people are watching', Hirschhorn warns. 'The rules are vague, there are a lot of grey areas, there are a lot less police around than in real life.'

Trader Monthly asked 2,500 traders on Wall Street in 2007: 'If you could use insider information in a $10 million trade, but had a 50 per cent chance of being caught, would you?' In response, 7 per cent said they would. If there was a 10 per cent chance of being arrested, 28 per cent would break the law. If there was no chance of being caught, 58 per cent would. So for 51 per cent of the traders, legality wasn't the problem. The problem was being caught breaking the law.

Partly this stems from traders being given a clear incentive to do the things that benefit them. It makes them fabulously rich. Every January, banks pay billions in bonuses to their traders. The outside world never understood why, but they didn't care too much. When we note that, despite the failure of the employers that these traders work for, we're still paying the bonuses, we start to wonder why.

An example: Goldman Sachs was saved by an injection of $10 billion of government money in October 2008. It received $12.9 billion as a consequence of the government bail out of AIG. It then announced pay and bonuses of $16.7 billion in pay and bonuses for the first three quarters of 2009.

One of the reasons for this type of behaviour, the banks counter, is that all the others are doing it. We need to hang on to our traders, and the traders hang on for cash.

'In this business titles, offices and the keys to the executive washroom are irrelevant, the only thing that matters is the number. You learn that effusive praise about your contribution translates into a lower number. … I have seen people so furious they have broken phones and punched holes in their screens with bare hands. I have seen people threaten their bosses', writes Satyajit Das in *Traders, Guns and Money.* 'Shareholders want higher profits; directors and chief executives want the stock to go up; if it is from trading profits, so be it. Traders are given every incentive to take risk and generate short-term profits.'

Too much testosterone

One way to improve the destructive behaviour of traders, most trader coaches agree, is not to give them rules to work around or regulations to covertly ignore. It's to employ more of an under-represented group.

'I think we should hire more women to be traders. Women are hard-wired to be better at trading. They are more open to criticism. Often men make a mistake and try to cover it, and that's when we get blow-ups', says Hirschhorn. One of the banks he consults for grades its traders. In the top 10 per cent, year after year, are around half of the women traders.

The difference, he explains, is that women do not consider losing a disaster, and so do not turn a small bad decision into a giant reckless one. They don't chase losses, they change their behaviour. Whether it's nature or nurture, it works. But banks tend to push women into sales, and don't encourage them to trade – because that's a job for the boys.

The gung-ho mentality of trading does not stop at the trading floor. The principle that there is supply and that supply is matched by demand, and that an efficient market is merely the one in which all the sellers and buyers are exposed to each other, creates efficiency in many situations. But in others, the idea that simply doing a deal solves your problem is dangerous.

One of those is the concept of 'opinion shopping'. In 2010, the report into Lehman Brothers' bankruptcy contained one major surprise: it had moved $50 billion of assets off its balance sheet, because this would lower its apparent leverage ratio. In effect, it made the bank seem safer than it was.[103]

The court-appointed examiner, Jenner & Block's Anton Valukas, said it was 'actionable balance sheet manipulation' and 'materially misleading', and that former CEO Richard Fuld was 'at least grossly negligent'. He pointed out in his report that internal e-mails described the process as a 'lazy way of managing the balance sheet as opposed to legitimately meeting balance sheet targets at quarter-end'.

It's the way that Lehman arrived at this strategy that interests us: its US outside counsel would not sign off on a treatment of loans, known as 'Repo 105', which magically made them into sales. So Lehman went shopping, and found its UK counsel willing to provide an opinion letter that this was a proper treatment of these assets. Lehman needed only one 'buyer' for its accounting practice. It couldn't sell it to local counsel, so it found a lawyer who could offer the opinion that it was within the rules. Opinion shopping is a problem in legal advice and also in auditing, where there may be a benefit in fees and status for firms who will go along. It is a type of trade: for Lehman, it outsourced ethical or legal questions. It traded them away.

Traders solve problems by trading them at the appropriate price. That's what they do.

In 2007, a lobbying group called Public Concern at Work raised a counterintuitive problem: there were, it claimed, too many whistleblowers in the City of London. Since the millennium there had been a 722 per cent rise in claims from redundant employees that they had lost their jobs because employers had discriminated against them for being whistleblowers – a claim for which, in law, the damages are theoretically limitless. For a trader, the compensation would have to reflect a period of unemployment at the previous salary – potentially, millions of pounds.

And overwhelmingly, the growth in complaints came from redundant traders. Other uncapped discrimination claims for race, sex or disability were more frequent, but a fraction of the increase in whistle-blowing claims. Few traders are non-white, female or disabled.

As an employment lawyer who works on behalf of one of the affected banks explained, to the affected traders it had become a form of parachute payment – one more win. If you think you might be made redundant from your trading desk, you go to HR and disclose, confidentially, that your colleagues are breaking the rules. Of course they are (see above), and of course a blind eye is turned to their behaviour (see above).

When you make this 'protected disclosure', no matter how trivial, you become a whistleblower. If you're told to clean your desk afterwards, your first call is to a lawyer who claims you have been victimized, and who can swiftly bump up your settlement – because no employer wants to face an employment tribunal based on how often, and how badly, its traders break the rules.

'For many of them,' she said, 'they're in their thirties, and it's time to get out. So this is one last, big trade.' This is the first, and the last, time in this book where investment banks might conceivably be victims.

Chapter Seven
Look what we made

Marriage is a wonderful invention: then again, so is a bicycle repair kit. BILLY CONNOLLY

There's plenty of evidence, by now, that most mergers don't work. Paul Butler of the Bureau of Economics Federal Trade Commission compares all the studies of the effects of mergers[104] for the two companies involved:

> When compared to industry share price indices or broad-based averages, mergers are often found to succeed less than half the time. In many cases transactions fail to enhance shareholder value (as measured against overall stock market performance, industry average returns, pre-merger trends, or a variety of other definitions)... Revenue growth is found to decline post-merger for both the target and the acquiring firm in a majority of cases.

There are plenty of reasons why mergers don't work that we have touched on earlier: one of the chief executive officers (CEOs) is dysfunctional. The two firms want to merge so much, they don't see that it's a terrible idea. They spend so much time merging that they forget what they're meant to be doing. Or, indeed, that the people paid to merge you are on such a huge bonus for completing, it would take a nuclear war to stop it.

Some mergers smell a bit from day one. Some bump along with a hidden problem which explodes a few months or years later. However they get there though, all the dysfunctional mergers throw both companies into reverse.

A fitting start to the 21st century
AOL Time Warner

On 11 January 2000, *The Times* in London reported on the 'Mega-deal that left seasoned market-watchers gasping': 'The title of most powerful man in the world may soon be taken away from Microsoft's Bill Gates and given to Steve Case, the head of America Online', it opened, adding that it was 'a fitting start to the 21st century... yet the scale and ambition of AOL's move still shocked the financial world.' At this point, we were gasping in a good way.

One of the most shocking aspects of the merger between AOL and Time Warner was who was buying whom: as AOL's stock price had ballooned in the previous two years, its market capitalization was much bigger than Time Warner's. The stock-only deal divided the companies so that AOL owned 55 per cent and the other 45 per cent was Time Warner – and even this undervalued AOL stock. The stock ticker symbol for the merged company would be 100 per cent AOL. Case got the chairman's job, with Gerald Levin, the CEO of Time Warner, as the merged company's nominal number two, the CEO.

Two and a half years later, the man who would have been the world's most powerful was resigning his chairman's job, pushed out by executives and shareholders alike. On 16 May 2003, Case used Winston Churchill's words about the 'end of the beginning' to mark his departure from the top job (the end of the end was to come soon, when Case resigned from the board). Five months after that, the story of the merger was complete – but not in a way that anyone would have predicted. AOL Time Warner changed its name back to Time Warner. AOL, once the senior partner in the merger, had become a business unit of one of the divisions of the company, and was perceived as such a drag on its reputation that its name was taken off the door.

In 2009 Time Warner announced that it was spinning off AOL into a stand-alone public company. The feverish optimism that had led Case, on the day of the merger, to predict that 'we're on the path of building what may be the most valuable company and most respected company in the world someday' had long since departed, as had the two CEOs who made it happen, and most of the fanciful ideas that were the justification for it. The merger of AOL and Time Warner is now seen as a benchmark for how not to create a mega-merger. It featured bad timing, bad luck, but most of all it was just a really, really bad idea.[105]

Synergies

The rationale for the merger was simple, but is perhaps the word used most often when people want to give a vague reason why two companies are better off together: synergy. Time Warner was a big, mature, stable business, based in the heart of New York. It owned *Time, People, Sports Illustrated*, Warner Brothers, Atlantic Records, HBO and CNN. It was vast, sprawling, and 20th century. It wasn't growing fast enough for the tastes of its shareholders or its CEO, and the popularly accepted reason for that at the time was: it didn't get the online thing.

This isn't unique for old-media businesses. The internet presented a challenge to films, music and TV that the industry is still trying to cope with, 11 years later. At the time, it seemed like the upstart new media companies would figure the whole problem out in a matter of months, provided they could find the time, so it was better to be inside their tent when they did.

AOL seemed to get the online thing better than anyone. Nine years earlier it had 150,000 subscribers, and in 2000 it had 34 million. In 1992 its IPO had raised $66 million and that felt like glorious wealth, but now its valuation was around 2,000 times that, and its employees owned sports cars and aeroplanes that they were barely old enough to drive and fly. Its revenues could not match an old media company's – even with AOL's aggressive sales culture, the combined company's revenues would be 80 per cent Time Warner, 20 per cent AOL – but that just showed how much more quickly AOL was destined to grow.

What was this synergy of which everyone spoke? It meant that by integrating AOL's internet exposure and Time Warner's brands, both became more valuable.[106] In the short term, it was accepted that Time Warner needed AOL more than AOL needed Time Warner. That's what the markets thought: the day of the merger, AOL stock slipped in value. Time Warner went up from $64.75 to $92.

The short version of the rationale for the merger was voiced by investment analyst David Readerman to the *New York Times* on the day of the merger: 'The nerds have won', he said. In more detail, it held out the possibility that Time Warner could cross-promote its TV and films on AOL. It meant that teams could sell advertising with an online, a TV and a magazine component. It meant that *Time* could find an online home which already had customers and readers and advertisers.

The year 2000 was the high watermark for this type of excitement, and the nerds showed little respect to old media – even old media in the same company. One dot-commer I interviewed was working for an online subsidiary of a multinational company, paid handsomely to come up with Big Ideas. When I asked him what it was like, he said it was like being in a little tugboat pulling an ocean liner out to sea, 'while desperately trying to saw through the rope'.

The dot-com kids like Case, who had created valuable online properties, appeared to have seen the future first. Old-school CEOs looked slow and unimaginative by comparison. AOL had better innovation, better marketing, better salesmen and more vision. If anything, its managers – almost all of whom knew nothing about the merger until it was announced – resented being held back by the dead weight of having to work with lazy traditional media people.

Yet, when it came to making the merger work, AOL ultimately presented many times more problems than tired old Time Warner.

Play nicely

The first, and most significant problem: how could Time Warner create synergies with AOL, when it couldn't even create synergies with itself? The company had been built so that its business units functioned independently. Their goal was to be the best in their market, not to find common ways to do business. They operated from different headquarters, with duplicated support functions, and no plans to change.

Time Warner's senior management also hadn't been blind to the potential of the internet, but it had just been unable to make it work. That was partly because the company was still bruised from the 1989 acquisition of Warner Brothers by Time, Inc. – two companies who worked alongside each other, rather than with each other.

Abortive attempts to create digital distribution of its content reached a nadir with the disastrous launch of Pathfinder, an early version of an internet portal, in October 1994. The idea was for the Pathfinder online service to use copy from all the Time Warner properties in a single destination. But Time Warner was a series of fiefdoms which wanted to do online their way, and couldn't see much benefit in sharing. Atlantic Records and Warner Brothers, for example, simply refused to be part of it. Inside Time Warner, Pathfinder people were known dismissively as the 'Nav Bar Nazis'.

When AOL's staff arrived five years later, they were not welcomed with open arms either. Partly this was because the staff often came from different generations. AOL people were young, brash, loud, casual, and had created a wild, rules-light culture. They felt rich, their stock options had made them fabulously wealthy before their careers had even started (though salaries were 50 per cent below the industry average) and many were aware that they didn't really need to work. They weren't accustomed to taking orders from people they didn't know.

On the other hand, Time Warner staff took salaries with small stock options, wore suits, and were often 20 years older. They had used those 20 years in one company to build up a pension and learn their trade. They valued their history and looked down on AOL's dot-commers. When it heard that some AOL staffers were coming to work in Time Warner's executive suite, senior staffers even took a selection of vintage film posters from the walls and hid them in storage, before the barbarians got hold of them.

So it's fair to say that there wasn't an abundance of trust coming from Time Warner to its new owners. Little did they know that the lack of trust was, in some cases, justified.

Off a cliff

Even before the merger was consummated, AOL's growth was proving tough to sustain. During the mid-1990s, AOL was originally designed to make revenue from the time that users spent online. When you signed up using one of AOL's billions of free disks, you then paid for each minute you spent using the service. AOL didn't have any advertising – nobody on the internet did that, because there weren't enough people to see the ads. Many of its subscribers would have found internet advertising a betrayal of the values of the internet.

Soon AOL switched to a flat-rate model, where you paid by the month. Users would stay on for hours, which slowed down the service and forced AOL to buy more servers and network capacity, and ate into its profits. But as subscriber numbers and minutes online mushroomed, it started to take advertising, and soon it found a lucrative source of revenue: the new generation of dot-com start-ups that were literally queuing up to give AOL their venture capital.

The early days of the dot-com boom ushered in a new model for business: it was wrong to make a profit too early in your existence. You needed customers, visitors to your website, word of mouth. Afterwards you could 'monetize' them. What mattered was your 'burn rate' – how fast you were using your cash to get to the next level.

AOL did a fantastic job of 'monetizing' the dot-coms. Its hyper-aggressive sales force would aim to get 50 per cent of the start-up's funding – not just its advertising budget. AOL hosted so many of the most valuable pages on the internet, and so many of the most valuable users – such as women and families – on the net were connected to AOL, that throwing millions into AOL made perfect sense to the dot-coms: if you're going to advertise online, do it with them.

By spring 1999, AOL had so much of the internet's advertising that it had a backlog of $1 billion of ads that were booked, but that it had not yet been able to run.

This couldn't last, and it didn't. By 1999 the dot-com revolution was running out of investment cash. Not only were there fewer big spenders putting their cash upfront, but some of those that had booked year-long campaigns were unable to pay. They had run out of funding and there was no more coming. As one official said afterwards, AOL salespeople used to say 'Destroy 'em. F*ck 'em.' They were, if anything, too good at doing that.

What outsiders, and Time Warner, didn't realize was that AOL's best growth was already behind it. AOL did the merger at the top of its ability to make the deal, because market sentiment would soon turn against AOL and most of its peers. AOL talked bravely of a 'flight to quality' when dot-com advertising went off a cliff. In reality it was a fall, not a flight.

Stop and wait

It might have seemed at the time of the merger announcement that AOL Time Warner would be starting the revolution immediately. This, too, was optimistic. A merger of this size between two media companies – one of which owned a cable TV network, and so had a means to provide internet service to homes which could freeze out rival ISPs – would attract the attention of regulators. The required regulatory clearance dragged on for a year and a day before the deal was approved. So the nerds won in the end, but they took a long time to do it. In the meantime, the company was in a state where it couldn't push ahead with any deep restructuring of two messy businesses, right at the time when restructuring was urgently needed.

The pressure to perform meant that AOL's business problems only got messier. The prediction when the merger was announced had been for double-digit growth. If it didn't make its revenue targets while the dot-com bubble was bursting, investor panic might have set in.

The pressure to make quarterly numbers had already pushed AOL into a series of what were known internally as 'BA specials', because they were handled by the business affairs team, which was the part of AOL that handled all the big deals. BA managed to make its targets every quarter, we know now, by an increasingly creative set of deals which it recognized as revenue even when no money changed hands. One example was a barter deal with Sun Microsystems, which had sold AOL $300 million of computers in 2000. AOL promised to buy $250 million more, as long as Sun purchased $37.5 million of advertising in the next three quarters. There was no cash behind this: Sun would give AOL a $37.5 million tab, to use in future. Barter deals like this were accounting for 10 per cent of revenues at the time, the limit set by management so they didn't become too obvious.

By September 2000, AOL internal figures showed it risked losing $108 million in booked revenue – mostly from failed, or failing, dot-coms. AOL kept this knowledge in-house, on the basis that it was small compared to the $2.7 billion in revenue it expected to make, and so did not need to be shared with investors. Also, AOL staff wanted to make its quarterly numbers at least until the merger was official. Unlike Time Warner, they had another year to wait for their stock to vest after the merger, and they took lower salaries and more stock. Any financial weakness would mean a falling stock price – effectively, lower pay.

Decline and fall

There were some synergy successes: but AOL had predicted tactical, strategic and transformational synergies, and the actual projects never got past the first level. Warner Music bundled AOL software. AOL sold magazine subscriptions. But even with this, and the unconventional financial deals (which would later see AOL restate $190 million in revenues for 2000 to 2002), there was no way that the merged company's growth targets could be met in 2001. Ironically, the worst-performing part of the company was now AOL. It had considered that Time Warner would be a brake on AOL's growth; the opposite was true.

In July 2001, the decline would become official. The company announced to investors that, unless trading picked up, it would need to lower its growth expectations for the fourth quarter. By the end of the year, Levin was ousted, and long-time Time Warner employee Richard Parsons took over. Later, Parsons would surround himself with fellow Time Warner executives, and announce that convergence and synergies were no longer a priority. But first he had to endure an annual shareholder meeting, where one investor told him that the deal, and the precious synergy, were 'pure hot air'. He added that shareholders had been 'conned into this'.

By the end of 2002, the most disastrous merger in the history of capitalism was all but dead. Shares were down 70 per cent, and the Time Warner lifers were looking at vastly reduced pensions. The company had taken write-downs at each end of the year which had meant that AOL Time Warner had lost $100 billion in 2002.

Washington Post reporter Alec Klein, who had followed the story for two years, quotes a Time Warner executive, speaking about AOL's financial weakness: 'They knew their ship was a piece of sh*t, it was so f*cking amazing it makes me sick... they did that to manipulate the deal. But when we pulled the hood up, it was too late.'

In three years, the dream of the world's most powerful company had died. It was a dream that was exaggerated by almost everyone in the press during the excitement of January 2000. 'There's no hyperbole about this deal', said the analyst at Deutsche Bank, when it was announced. 'At every stage in AOL's phenomenal growth, Case has been coldly realistic about the assets he had in hand', was *USA Today*'s verdict.

Salomon Smith Barney had created a valuation for the merger which was extremely precise, but not at all accurate: in 2001, it predicted, $6 billion advertising revenues would become $9 billion, even without the fabled synergies.

All, for reasons that became obvious very soon afterwards, couldn't have been more wrong.

Breaking up is hard to do
Royal Bank of Scotland and ABN AMRO

In October 2006, the FTSE reached its highest level since 2001. Yet one of its stars in that period was, in the perception of investors, running out of steam.

Royal Bank of Scotland (RBS) had spent most of the previous 279 years as a small, innovative but conservative bank. It had, among other things, invented the mortgage as we know it. But by the year 2000 it was ambitious and driven, in the image of Sir Fred Goodwin, its CEO.

'Fred the Shred', as we now know him, made his reputation through a series of acquisitions[107] – and one in particular. On 14 February 2000 RBS bought its competitor NatWest for £21 billion, in a hostile takeover that snatched the prize from its Scottish rival Bank of Scotland, who made their own disastrous merger afterwards as a result, which we'll get to. Even NatWest management were opposed to the deal, but Sir Fred pushed it through, and managed to integrate the two organizations brilliantly afterwards.

Two years later, RBS had become the fifth-largest bank in the world by market capitalization. *Forbes* magazine had named him its businessman of the year. RBS's acquisition strategy moved up a gear. It acquired another 20 companies in four years. The deals were known for being carefully plotted and priced, with cost-cutting efficiencies ruthlessly executed (hence 'the shred', as redundant ex-employees would confirm).

And yet the share price faltered. Analysts were worried that the bank was doing too many deals, and that it would be so distracted by the effort to integrate its purchases that it would lose sight of its existing customers.

On the other hand, the banking industry in 2006 was simultaneously booming and consolidating. Having got to number five, RBS would need to grow rapidly to stay there.

Not big enough

It was a problem faced by Dutch bank ABN AMRO at the same moment. Having grown rapidly through the 2000s by global acquisitions, by the beginning of 2007 it was a top 10 bank in Europe, based on its assets, and in the top 15 worldwide. It had branches in 53 countries, which was impressive for a bank which had been formed in 1974 by the merger of the two largest Dutch commercial banks. On the other hand, executives knew that growth had stalled. ABN AMRO had set out to be a top five bank too, but without a partner it wouldn't get there.

Others had noticed: on 27 November 2006, in a 40-page note, analysts at Citigroup speculated that it would be a good deal for both ABN AMRO and RBS if RBS were to acquire its competitor, but that the deal would be unlikely to happen. Nevertheless: 'We are not saying RBS would buy ABN Amro, but... we believe RBS potentially should buy ABN Amro', Citigroup said, paying £36 billion, and making synergies of £1.8 billion.

Momentum was building for ABN AMRO to make a deal. It hadn't been as effective in its acquisitions, and investors, including the hedge fund TCI, were calling for the group to be broken up. Instead, it started talks to merge with Barclays, which it made exclusive, and public, in March 2007.

Sir Fred had promised to stop buying banks: its shareholders wanted dividends and organic growth. So one month later, a consortium of three banks led by RBS had retaliated with a hostile counter-bid that was 10 per cent higher. The consortium wanted to break up the group between themselves, and dispose of some of the other assets, which had been poorly integrated into the group. ABN AMRO still wanted to do the deal with Barclays, but shareholders, led by TCI, didn't.

There was, however, a bigger force at work in the market during 2007. 'Sub-prime is definitely there at the forefront of everyone's mind and it's not going away', said Marc Ostwald, bond analyst at Monument Securities, in July, when we first started to hear the term 'credit crunch'. US Federal Reserve chairman Ben Bernanke had told a US congressional hearing that sub-prime mortgage losses could hit $100bn, which now seems almost comically low as an estimate. Nevertheless, it was enough to spook the markets.

RBS had agreed to pay not £36 million for ABN AMRO, but £47 million. While other banks, seeing problems ahead, cancelled acquisition strategies and concentrated on survival, RBS ploughed on. 'People who do win pay more than people who don't win', Sir Fred had told the *International Herald Tribune* on 10 October 2007, five days after Barclays had thrown in the towel and handed the victory to RBS.

But RBS shares were already falling: with concerns about its exposure to sub-prime, and worries about whether it had overpaid, its shares fell back to levels last seen in 2000 – and continued to plunge.

For the first time it occurred to investors: did having a global structure really deliver the synergies that were promised? Standard & Poor's pointed out that exactly the reason that ABN AMRO was being broken up was that it had been unable to find efficiencies in its leading-edge global payments system.

Yearly profits of £10bn announced in December 2007 came with reassurance: Sir Fred said it was 'fashionable to think there's going to be unpleasantness in the future', but that he was optimistic – because he had now built, yes, a global business.

Man or megalomaniac?

Europe largest cross-border deal, and the largest-ever financial services acquisition, turned out to be the deal that terminally weakened RBS as a publicly owned bank. Faced with a weak balance sheet, RBS announced a £15 billion share issue to raise funds in 2008. Just 0.24 per cent of the shares were taken up. Instead, the government was forced to do its own acquisition – 57.9 per cent of RBS, a rescue described by Sir Fred as a 'drive-by shooting'. He left soon afterwards, having earned £30 million in salary in his time as CEO, with an £8.4 million pension pot.

We don't yet know if the government did a better deal with RBS than ABN AMRO had done. It didn't start well. In January 2009, RBS announced the largest loss in British banking history – more than £7 billion.

Two factors, by common consent, broke the well-oiled RBS acquisition machine. The first was a lack of due diligence. While RBS acquisitions had always been plotted by a small band of advisers, Sir Fred's reputation was built on a thorough analysis, which set the right price, and allowed him to commit or walk away with confidence that he was doing the right thing.

Yet in a presentation to analysts on 29 May 2007, board member Johnny Cameron had told analysts that 'Quite a few people have been through ABN AMRO and joined us or know ABN AMRO well. It's remarkable how much you can gain from external analysis around the world.' He added that: 'then we had the one meeting in the Netherlands... and had some conversation with [board member Pierre Overmars] about his business. I have to say the one reaction I came away with was, if anything, our bottom up looks like an underestimate.' This sounded like a company that was no longer giving attention to detail – either because it wanted to do the deal too badly, or because it had lost the ability to criticize itself.

The other problem, with hindsight, was Sir Fred. He had become banking's celebrity, and some of his investors thought that he cared more about his bank being big than being efficient. As long ago as 2005, James Eden of Dresdner Kleinwort Wasserstein told Sir Fred, in a meeting with analysts, that 'some of our investors think Sir Fred is a megalomaniac who cares more about size than shareholder value'.

RBS was a broken bank, but Sir Fred is not a broken man. Controversially, he appeared in front of a House of Commons committee, with other senior bankers, in February 2009 to explain the failure. Memorably, having masterminded the worst acquisition in banking history for which British taxpayers had picked up the tab, he apologized for the failings of his bank rather than any personal misjudgements. Afterwards *The Times* 'Bugle' podcast gave the opinion that 'there wasn't a single person in that room who wouldn't have seriously benefitted from a slap across the face'. Sir Fred's apology, it added, was 'not so much half-a*sed as containing barely-perceptible traces of buttock'.

Shooting the messenger
Bank of Scotland and Halifax

The whistleblower's role, both in the UK and in the United States, is protected by law. If you uncover unwise or potentially criminal conduct, and disclose this, you are protected by law if your employer decides to shoot the messenger. This is one of the arguments in favour of self-regulation: that the officers of a company can police themselves better than an outside regulator, because members of staff are effectively investigating from the inside 24 hours a day, secure in the knowledge that their job is not in danger if their bosses don't like what they hear.

Yet the story of the demise of HBoS, once the UK's fifth-largest bank, centres on the investigations of its own risk manager – and the warnings from him that were ignored because, following a £28 billion merger of two entirely different organizations, one corporate culture came to dominate another.

Coming into the financial crisis, HBoS was not seen as a weak bank: it held more mortgages than any other bank in the UK; it combined two brands – Bank of Scotland (BoS) and Halifax – which were powerful reminders that banking wasn't invented to make traders rich, but to help ordinary people; and it was consistently and aggressively profitable.

That aggression would ultimately force the group into a shotgun marriage to save itself in 2008, with the British prime minister holding the shotgun. Only afterwards did we hear from the risk manager who tried to blow the whistle, and could potentially have saved the independence of the group. We didn't hear what he had to say when it could have helped, because when he discovered the rottenness at the heart of HBoS he was made redundant by the same trusted colleagues who had sent him to investigate. He was also ignored by the banking regulator, the organization that, for public consumption, championed the role of internal risk managers.

Paul Moore, the whistleblower in question, had warned the board over the bad business practices, a direct result of a merger which had led to a runaway risk-taking culture, six years earlier. The board, many of whom had been among the UK's most conservative administrators before the merger, could have reformed the bank. Instead it chose to shoot the messenger.

Red-meat culture

Both banks had a distinguished history. The Governor and Company of the Bank of Scotland, created in 1695, was the second-oldest bank in the world. The Bank of England, its only predecessor, was set up to finance military operations. In England, the South Seas Company was created to finance business speculation, and look how that ended. In Scotland, the Bank was set up specifically to help businesspeople get access to the investment they needed. It issued – and still issues – Scottish banknotes, competed fiercely with its younger sibling the Royal Bank of Scotland, and reached the 1990s with three centuries of unbroken strength and respect. The two big Scottish banks were, at the time, almost comically conservative in their outlook, but BoS wasn't about to go making the crazy speculations that had brought down many of its smaller rivals in the past 300 years.

The Halifax Permanent Benefit Building and Investment Society was founded in 1853, as part of the Victorian building society movement. Mutually owned, it shared the profits of its business among all its investors, and existed to help ordinary working people afford a house in which to live. During the 1980s and 1990s, when many building societies combined or collapsed, Halifax grew more slowly – but by the turn of the century was the UK's largest mortgage lender.

One factor changed the direction of these two great institutions: the deregulation and subsequent expansion of British banking through the 1990s. BoS was looking for an English partner; Halifax Building society demutualized, becoming a public limited company in 1997. It gradually replaced its steady growth with a red-meat sales culture as it expanded into current accounts, loans and retail banking.

When they announced a merger on 4 May 2001, Halifax was not BoS's first choice, nor was it the natural fit that executives routinely claim for mergers. Recent expansion had made Halifax twice as large as its Scottish partner, and there was no doubt who was in the driving seat: the merged entity initially offered the top three jobs in HBoS to Halifax executives. 'For two years the Bank of Scotland has been wafting around like a spare sock at the back of the drawer, looking for a partner. We all know about two of its failed deals – with National Westminster and Abbey National – but there have been plenty of others', wrote Neil Bennett in a withering blast in the *Sunday Telegraph*.[108] 'The spin machines were set on overdrive on Friday when the Halifax and BoS announced their "merger". A quick reading of the press release reveals that this was the sort of "merger" Germany offered Poland in 1939.'

A walk in the park

Yet BoS still managed to reassert its status. After the merger was complete, Sir James Crosby became chief executive. A BoS lifer, he wasn't in a rush to throw away BoS's long tradition. He complained to journalists – when their pens were in their pockets – that his venerable bank had sold out to a common building society.

Below him, that tradition was quickly subsumed. The headquarters of the merged group might have been in Edinburgh, but the character of the new organization was definitely created in Halifax. Doubts over the business practices of Halifax's sales culture surfaced in public in 2003, when the BBC *Money Programme* screened a documentary that pointed to widespread HBoS-related mortgage fraud. Brokers who gave business to HBoS were advising applicants (in this case, undercover journalists) to lie on their applications, which would inevitably be accepted by salespeople incentivized to write as many loans as possible.[109] A fast-track loan approval process was also vulnerable to liars. 'Just remember what you put on the form and make sure the mortgage is always paid', said a mortgage broker on the programme. 'It's a walk in the park. They don't know.' Sir James refused to be interviewed by the programme.

Behind the scenes, Paul Moore, the head of regulatory risk at the bank, was an independent thinker who didn't like the direction the bank was taking: the traditional bankers seemed to be in awe of the salespeople who were growing the business so quickly. 'There is an inherent requirement at times for people who do risk management and compliance to present the contrary view to groupthink', he told a BBC interviewer in 2009.[110] 'But people find it very difficult to accept feedback that they don't want to hear. It's human nature.'

In 2002 and 2003 he recalls that 'I already had sufficient evidence to know that things were pretty pacy in the Halifax'. The dramatic sales growth was boosting group profits, but 'the trouble was, like all good ideas, it went too far'. To encourage the sales culture, controls had been relaxed in the division, leading to the sort of lax risk management that the reporters had uncovered. What might have been a disciplinary offence in the previous era was now – out of sight of the managers – commonplace.

In an internal review, Moore recalls that he was shocked by how far this had been allowed to embed itself in a bank that was desperate to make up ground on HSBC, Barclays, Lloyds TSB and RBS, the 'Big Four' British banks.

By November 2003, the Financial Services Authority (FSA), the banks' regulator, was writing to HBoS to warn that it 'had assessed key parts of the Group as posing high or medium-high risks to the achievement of its statutory objectives of maintaining market confidence and protecting consumers.'

Moore records that the letter said that: 'There has been evidence that development of the control function in Retail Division has not kept pace with the increasingly sales driven operation...' and 'There is a risk that the balance of experience amongst senior management could lead to a culture which is overly sales focused and gives inadequate priority to risk issues.'

The pressure cooker

At the time, the Chairman of the Retail Risk Control Committee was non-executive director Charles Dunstone, the CEO of Carphone Warehouse, who was an expert in growing a high-street sales operation, but had no experience in banking or financial risk management. He was also a personal friend of the man who was the chief executive of the retail banking operation (and also a man whose previous experience was in high-street retail rather than finance), Andy Hornby.

It fell to Moore to look closely at how the Halifax retail sales culture had unbalanced the organization. His department conducted 50 management and 140 staff interviews, and he recalls it was 'like taking the lid off a pressure cooker'. One employee told him that 'We'll never hit our sales targets and sell ethically'.

Some managers resented what they considered to be meddling from the compliance department. One leaned across the table to Moore during his interview: 'I'm warning you, don't make a f*cking enemy out of me', he said.

To the old hands who had built the Bank of Scotland, rather than run supermarkets and mobile phone stores, this should have been shocking: but it was hardly a secret. Moore had discovered that the bank had, under the surface, 'a culture of fear if you didn't hit your targets... It was pervasive. It was throughout. The entire organization was focused on selling, selling, selling, but not on risk management. It flabbergasted me.'

What flabbergasted him more was when, after raising the concerns strongly in his report (and initially being congratulated), he was suddenly made redundant without warning, in person, by one of those old-style bankers. Sir James Crosby replaced Moore with an employee with no formal experience in financial risk management. Moore warned the FSA about his concerns, but when they took no action he despaired of being able to change the culture. He eventually reached a financial settlement (with accompanying gagging order) with HBoS.

Fast forward four years, and HBoS was learning the cost of its aggressive sales culture: in March 2008 there were rumours (false ones, but widely believed at the time) that the bank had asked for emergency funding. Hedge funds were rumoured to be short-selling HBoS because of the risk of default on its loan portfolio, which suddenly looked wildly risky. On 17 September 2008, the day after the failure of Lehman Brothers, there was wild speculation about how deep the HBoS exposure to credit risk was. Aside from Royal Bank of Scotland, HBoS looked the most vulnerable of the high-street banks, thanks to all those mortgages.

Bailing out

The gossip sent its share price into freefall: eventually we would find out that the gossip was at least partly justified, because in February 2009 HBoS's new owner announced that the bank had made a pre-tax loss of £10.8 billion in 2008 – £1.6 billion more than even the most pessimistic estimates had suggested.

The Bank of England and the UK government were not prepared to let HBoS collapse, but it couldn't survive unaided. To save the UK banking industry, HBoS was swallowed by Lloyds TSB, one of the 'Big Four' that it was trying to unseat. A combination of a Lloyds TSB takeover (without the need for regulatory approval that would have made such a deal impossible in normal times) and a 40 per cent stake from the British government avoided a probable collapse, which might have dragged many other banks down with it.

HBoS had made a desperate gamble to be huge, but had thrown away the ideals that had made both parts of the business successful for a combined life of 500 years in the frantic race to the top. It could not cope with the salesmanship that it thought would bring it success. Instead, it got rid of the whistleblower who told the truth about what had happened.

'Being an internal risk and compliance manager at the time felt a bit like being a man in a rowing boat trying to slow down an oil tanker', Moore later told the Treasury Select Committee.[111] 'Anyone whose eyes were not blinded by money, power and pride, who really looked carefully knew there was something wrong and that economic growth based almost solely on excessive consumer spending based on excessive consumer credit based on massively increasing property prices which were caused by the very same excessively easy credit could only ultimately lead to disaster.'[112]

To infinity, and beyond *USWeb*

The dot-com era is a rich source of companies that were almost revolutionary, many now forgotten, because the genius children broke their toys, and had them taken away when the grown-ups came home. Remember USWeb? No, not many people do.

The Industry Standard described USWeb's growth strategy in May 1998: 'Since March 1997, it has bought 26 companies, paying for the acquisitions with options and shares currently worth some $200 million. For this the company has been well rewarded. Its stock, which opened at $10 a share in a December 1997 public offering, is now worth more than $22 (a few months ago, it reached a peak of nearly $40). Meanwhile, revenues have climbed from $0 in 1996 to just under $14 million in the last quarter.'[113]

The strategy was driven by CEO Joe Firmage, who at this time was 27 years old. 'Find a company with expertise in developing corporate intranets and extranets. Look at the balance sheet. Put an offer on the table and don't negotiate too much – base only 25 percent of the offer on subjective elements like the perceived strength of the management team', he told the writer.

Soon after this was published I met Firmage and his young management team, who could best be described as euphoric, having just pulled off their biggest acquisition of all. USWeb had swallowed one of its rivals, CKS, who had also been on an acquisition binge. The firm was now a 1,950-person company with a market valuation of $2.1 billion. It was working for Apple Computer, Levi Strauss and Harley-Davidson, among others. Firmage was one of the heroes of the revolution, and almost no one questioned the wisdom of two aspects of this strategy:

1 USWeb built websites, which was a widely available skill. As Philip Kaplan, the founder of website F*ckedCompany.com commented at the time, 'Not only did web shops like USWeb/CKS convert a lot of suckers into paying customers, but they fooled the media, which in turn fooled the general public.'

2 The strategy worked only as long as the share price kept climbing. It wasn't so much a strategy as a momentum. The acquisitions were not done with hard cash, but with stock. So you acquire, your evident genius causes investors to buy into your company (see point 1), your share price grows, the acquired staff (who were paid in shares) are

delighted, and both factors make it easier to do another acquisition, which increases your obvious genius, and so on, 26 times.

How long can a strategy like this go on? Companies like Cisco have grown almost entirely by acquisition. Much of Microsoft's best technology was bought, because when Microsoft says it wants to buy you, you really don't have a choice. Both of them, however, were selling things that other companies couldn't do. USWeb was most definitely not.

There was, it turns out, something else too. I didn't know it at the time, but I was present at one of the final scenes of the drama. On the day we met, Firmage was excellent company. We were scheduled to go for lunch, but the meeting spread into the evening. He and his colleagues ordered Cuban cigars and cognac, and we went to a Soho jazz club. I asked him every question in my head and filled half a notebook.

An important question

There was one question, however, I didn't ask. That question was: 'Do you believe that aliens have visited earth and passed on some of their technological secrets to the entrepreneurs of Silicon Valley thus giving them an advantage in their research and development processes, and indeed do you believe they have visited you?' Had I asked this, Firmage would have answered: 'Yes.'

And had I followed up with 'You should really publish some kind of document about this', he would have said that this was exactly what he was about to do, that it was 600 pages long, and he was about to post it on the internet. When you've done 26 acquisitions in a couple of years, finding the time to write this up speaks of a commitment. Previously entranced investors, however, began to doubt the direction in which that commitment was being channelled.

By January 1999, Firmage's career as the boss of a multibillion-dollar company was over. He resigned from the board of the merged operation after competitors started to make fun of his reputation as a management genius, what with the extra-terrestrial thing and all. Which, both Firmage and new CEO Robert Shaw admitted, were damaging the company.[114]

On the back of Firmage's spree, the company had pulled off one more mega-merger, joining with a traditional management consultancy called Whittman-Hart. The combined entity reached, in the dot-com frenzy, a market cap of $14 billion – about the same as BMW. And then, just as quickly, it collapsed. Revenues were far too small to sustain this valuation, and fees for clients (for website-building jobs that many realized they could do quite easily themselves for a fraction of the price) too high. Once the aura of genius had departed, and the valuation with it, the remaining assets were sold off for $60 million.

Firmage is still an entrepreneur, and probably still excellent company in a jazz club. With hindsight, he wasn't a genius, the company he built wasn't worth a great deal, and there's obviously the, you know, other thing, which he still believes. If he ever proves it, will my face ever be red! Still wouldn't have made USWeb's strategy a good idea though.

When mergers go bad

There is now a large and rapidly growing literature on how bad mergers can be. And yet we don't fall out of love with them:

- Thirty per cent of IT projects run late, which is a scandalous waste of money.
- About half of all new marriages end in divorce, which is a depressing indictment of our inability to commit.
- Three out of five felons are repeat offenders, which clearly shows that prison doesn't rehabilitate them.

And yet these numbers are excellent when you compare them to the figures on mergers and acquisitions (M&A). A survey of 193 mergers by Southern Methodist University[115] showed that only 36 per cent of them maintained revenue growth after one quarter, and 89 per cent suffered a slowdown by the end of three quarters. McKinsey researched 160 acquisitions, and only one in eight managed to accelerate their growth inside three years. The acquirers had growth rates 4 per cent lower than their peers who hadn't gone through M&A.

The *Journal of Finance* studied acquiring firms: they suffered an average 10 per cent wealth loss over five years, and between 40 and 55 per cent broke down. A study in the *Harvard Business Review* found that, of mergers between 1993 and 1997, 48 per cent had failed in less than 24 months.[116]

If M&A was a horse, they'd shoot it. Every study of the effectiveness of M&A across the board shows that, on average, it destroys money. And yet, there's a lot of it going on, hobbling perfectly good, separate, companies in search of benefits that will never be realized.

Partly this is because it's easy to find a question for which M&A is an answer. When growth is strong, you acquire to outpace your rivals (during the boom period from 1996 to 2001, there were $12 trillion of acquisitions – about one an hour). When there's a downturn, you should acquire because there are companies that are cheap. If you want to grow market share, acquire a competitor. If you want to diversify, buy a company that isn't a competitor.

There are more problems with M&A than would fill a book, but there are two that concern us here: the cult of acquisition, and must-buy overexcitement.

I want one of those

It's in the interests of a lot of people to do the deal, and of relatively few not to. M&A, once begun, has a natural momentum.

Firstly, because it provides a way to do the most basic function of a company: to grow. Not just to grow market share, but reach the level of expertise in the company, and reputation. These things take a long time to develop organically. Buying them as a job lot is a way to solve the problem of success: once your shareholders demand growth in every quarter, what can you do? Problem: you'll get a big bump in quarter zero, you have the illusion of growth – but the two companies together will usually still be short of where they would have been had they entered an alliance or partnership.

But no one likes alliances because they're not fun. They are full of people arguing and wanting to slice off more of the profits for themselves. And the CEO's not going to get on the cover of *Business Week* under the headline: 'Carefully analysed partnerships with strategic partners create a better business'. Not when there is the deal of the century being signed once an hour.

Second, once you go some way down the road, and the other firm is flirting, some other firm might decide to get involved. So then it's not a question of whether you acquire or not – if you don't, chances are your competitor will. So then there's a bidding war, and you raise your offer and win, and you just paid 20 per cent more than you thought you were going to have to. You've just won a deal that guarantees you'll not make any money. It's known as the Winner's Curse.[117]

The Winner's Curse was discovered by three oil company engineers in the 1950s, who wondered why exploration was not more profitable. It turned out that the process by which the companies bid for drilling rights caused the problem. As the rights went to the most optimistic bidder, the contracts tended to overestimate the value of the oil in the ground. The middle bidder would most likely have assigned the right price – but the middle bidder never wins.

You can test it yourself by auctioning a jar of coins. The winner will usually overestimate the value of the coins, and so makes a loss.

One of the best examples of the Winner's Curse causing fit-to-bustness: Robert Campeau, whose Campeau Corporation in the 1980s used junk bonds to achieve leveraged buyouts of US retailers at what seemed, even at the time, any price. He bought Allied Stores, and then in 1988 Federated Department Stores – best known as the owner of Bloomingdale's. He outbid R.H. Macy & Company, and paid $6.6 billion. By January 1990, Bloomingdale's was literally surviving week by week as Campeau's debts meant he struggled to pay suppliers. As one of them told *Time Magazine*: 'After a while, it became a contest of wills and ego. Campeau came to feel that it was a game and he had to win the prize.'

Or, as *The New York Times* put it: 'Any corporate executive can figure out how to file for bankruptcy when the bottom drops out of the business. It took the special genius of Robert Campeau, chairman of the Campeau Corporation, to figure out how to bankrupt more than 250 profitable department stores.'[118]

Of course, once you've started an acquisition, it's suddenly in a lot of people's interests not to walk away. There are literally thousands of consultants and bankers whose life, sorry 'yacht', depends on the deal getting done. As soon as there's a fee on the table, the CEO will never get truly neutral advice again.

Must buy

Related to this: the desire of managers, and the CEO especially, to do the big deal. It's the ultimate test. Pull this one off, and you're a hero. Not just among your pals, but in the press, on TV. The positive news, 'we did the deal', comes on one glorious day. The negative, 'the deal's falling apart because they hate us and we hate them', dribbles out over months. Success makes a big splash. Failure is a hushed affair by comparison. It lends an unrealistic balance to M&A reporting. The optimistic, but untested, marketing twaddle drowns out the pragmatic voices of experience. It makes the entire industry seem more exciting and successful than it really is:

> When capital is extensively available and companies are busy doing deals, some executives start behaving like bluefish. Doing deals is exciting. Making one's company bigger is thrilling… when the investment banker calls with a prospect, the executive bites.

Many deals fall into this category… the quality of thinking, preparation and post-merger management is inferior. Once in a while, the result is a success. But the reason is luck combined with superior scrambling by the acquirer.

So said Joseph Bower, a professor of Business Administration at Harvard Business School in 'Not all M&As are alike, and that matters', a paper published in 2001. More research on the topic: 'Because acquisitions increase the size of a firm, they also have a positive effect on a top executive's compensation, and enhance his/her power.'

The result: a refusal to walk away, and that means either overpaying, or not doing the merger at all. The average premium in a merger over the share price is between 40 and 50 per cent. That's putting a lot of pressure on the ability to synergize – a pressure that the CEO is blind to: 'When hubris is instrumental in the acquisition, it is not uncommon for the CEO to do a less than adequate job of due diligence or to ignore negative information provided by the due diligence process.'[119]

In seven out of 10 cases, the acquired firm never delivers the synergies to justify the premium. Especially when the company didn't want to be acquired.

Aspiration is a wonderful thing: but few companies have the ability to acquire successfully. Doesn't stop them trying, though.

Chapter Eight
Almost revolutionary

> *We all agree your theory is crazy. The question is whether it's crazy enough to have a chance of being correct.*
>
> **NEILS BOHR, PHYSICIST**

We've been making fun of people with crazy ideas ever since someone had the crackpot idea that if you rubbed two sticks together you could make fire. As if. Daniel Defoe was making fun of the inventors of his day when he wrote *Gulliver's Travels* in 1726. When Gulliver visited the island of Laputa, a place where science flourished but no one had the first idea what to do with it, he visited a group (modelled on the Royal Society, the dot-com kids of his day) called the Society of Projectors:

> The first Man I saw was of a meager Aspect, with sooty Hands and Face, his Hair and Beard long, ragged and singed in several Places. His Cloathes, Shirt, and Skin were all of the same Colour. He had been Eight Years upon a Project for extracting Sun-Beams out of Cucumbers, which were to be put into Vials hermetically sealed, and let out to warm the Air in raw inclement Summers. He told me he did not doubt in Eight Years more he should be able to supply the Governors Gardens with Sun-shine at a reasonable Rate.

Later, he encounters a workshop where he was 'almost overcome with a horrible Stink', because the inventor was embarked on a project to 'reduce human Excrement to its original Food, by separating the several Parts, removing the Tincture which it receives from the Gall, making the Odour exhale, and scumming off the Saliva'. An architect was busy devising a scheme to build houses, starting at the roof.

We've got a pretty low threshold for revolutionaryness these days, thanks in part to an overheated marketing department which is only too happy to declare every new product a 'revolution'. Saying that's just a new thing to buy seems too ordinary. We need to be entertained and flattered if we're going to break out the credit card, and making us part of the revolution in mobile handset design or breathable underwear does both.

At the other end of the scale, there are some brilliant people who create a revolution that, in the phrase coined by Georg Büchner, 'devours its own children': AIG and LTCM are good examples. And there are some revolutions that are just silly. Any history of the birth of the internet throws up hundreds. They're funny – but somewhere along the dead-end road to the revolution, someone's lost their house.

Genius and craziness in business are closer than we like to think. Not least because it's really hard to tell the geniuses that they're crazy when they are, hitherto, richer and more successful than you. It's also tough to say that the revolution is crazy when it appears to be making millionaires out of everyone who gets involved in it. It's hardest of all to tell the revolutionary he's crazy when the revolutionary is your boss.

Enhanced securitization *AIG*

On 18 March 2009, American International Group, Inc. (AIG) sent out a memo to its staff with the title 'Enhanced Security Notification'. It isn't the usual memo that you send to a group of insurance underwriters: 'Due to a growing sense of public attention fueled by increased media scrutiny, AIG Corporate Security would like to highlight increased security measures...', it began. The memo warned AIG staff not to wear AIG-branded clothing, to hide their badges, to look out for locks that have been tampered with in their office and not to prop doors open, not to talk about being an AIG employee in public, and even 'At night, when possible, always travel in pairs and park in well lit areas.'[120]

On bulletin boards, employees responded to a memo warning them not to go out alone with frustration, one talking about colleagues who were: 'literally shaking as they go to work in the morning, worried that some nutbar will show up with an uzi... Oh, and resignation won't help much either – AIG's turning out to be the kiss of death on a resume.'

This, at what had been the 18th-largest public company in the world, and certainly one of the top 10 most boring. At least, that's how it seemed on the surface. In one small part of one division of AIG, things had got pretty racy in the 10 years prior to AIG staff becoming public enemy number one. The incidents that led AIG's employees to fear a lynching had mostly benefitted, and been caused by, a group of 377 employees in a London offshoot, who had found a business that they thought couldn't fail. The lust for growth at almost any price, tacitly approved by a management who clearly did not understand the risk they were taking on, gave them carte blanche to destroy the company for their personal gain. And, many argue, it's AIG that is mainly responsible for almost bringing down the world's financial system with it.

AIG didn't go bust in the conventional sense. It's still out there, seeking buyers for its assets and gradually unwinding its positions, protected by $185 billion of US government money.

That's right – $185 billion. Even in the context of the bank bail outs of 2008, AIG scooped the pot. In return, the US government got 79.9 per cent of the company, and AIG employees got death threats.

We know where you live

The threats weren't just about the bail out, though it did serve to focus the minds of the sort of crazy people who threaten violence against innocent office workers. It wasn't just that AIG's shares had crashed, costing investors who had delighted in its superficial combination of growth and stability many thousands of dollars. It wasn't even that AIG was the fulcrum of the machine that crashed the global financial system, ruining thousands more or taking their jobs and houses. It was mainly that, after all this, the company paid $165 million of its government bail out money straight back to the employees who were responsible – as performance bonuses.

It's fair to say that the staff responsible for the crash hadn't quite come round to the point of view that it was all their fault. The cultish belief that they had created a wonderful money machine with zero risk proved persistent, even in the face of evidence to the contrary.

If you were thinking of something that might, possibly, inflame public opinion, you'd be hard pressed to come up with anything better than the behaviour of AIG management. Some of the bonus money was recovered after New York Attorney General Andrew Cuomo obtained the names and addresses of the recipients, and – in a spirit of public-spiritedness, rather than crude populism – threatened to make them public. The 'we know where you live' approach to negotiation made $50 million, though it prompted some executives in the AIG London office, which had made most of the fabulous profits and directly caused the largest quarterly loss in corporate history, to report Cuomo to the UK's equivalent of the FBI.

Reuters reported: '[A] compliance officer for the Banque AIG unit in London went so far as to ask UK authorities from the Serious Organised Crime Agency (SOCA) to probe whether demands to return the payments could be considered extortion, according to emails.'[121] One executive told Reuters that the requests to return the money were 'blackmail', adding, 'There is no moral reason to give it back.' AIG's financial products people might have been short on humility, but they were long on self-confidence.

AIG was born in Shanghai in 1919. Slow, steady growth was speeded up in the 1980s and 1990s by expansion and innovation, especially in insuring credit risks that had sprung up thanks to the explosion in derivatives, which packaged those risks so they could be traded.

AIG's dash for growth had also run into trouble over the techniques it used to make its balance sheet more exciting. There were secret agreements with customers – most notably General Re, which had paid $500 million in premiums for AIG to insure a $500 million risk, which didn't exist. This boosted AIG's balance sheet by $500 million in that year. A former executive at General Re pleaded guilty to a conspiracy to misstate AIG's finances in 2005, and also in 2005, AIG restated the last five years of financial statements: its income had been exaggerated by $3.9 billion.

The fault isn't solely with AIG. The expectations of success are that it doesn't slow down, but that's a problem if you sell insurance. There comes a point at which everything that can be insured is insured. Other firms create new types of insurance – so you create products that will insure the insurance. It provides growth, but also builds a precarious infrastructure with risks worth trillions of dollars.

New business

AIG needed a new business to keep up growth, and derivatives would provide it. In 1987, Joseph Cassano had set up AIG Financial Products (AIGFP) in London, in Mayfair.[122] It was largely autonomous, and worked as a hedge fund would: taking large financial risks in the derivatives market, then taking opposite risks, and pocketing the difference whatever happened. In the late 1990s, AIGFP was convinced by JP Morgan salespeople that it should write insurance for the mortgage-backed derivatives that were becoming so popular. These derivatives, named 'collateralized debt obligations', or CDOs, were basically ignored by the wider world, including financial regulators, but had made millions for investors who were trading them. In 2007, there were about $57 trillion of unregulated derivatives similar to CDOs. A CDO took thousands of mortgages, threw all the debt together, and packaged them up. As mortgages were mostly sound investments, and low-risk ones, a derivative made from them was a low-risk proposition. In a housing boom, banks could write more mortgages, and sell the debt as CDOs to other banks.

CDOs were considered, at first, to be almost risk-free, and many were rated AAA – as good as credit gets. They were backed by something real: houses. As your parents told you, you never lose money on a house. If a few homeowners defaulted on their loan, the banks got the house instead. Nothing short of a collapse in the housing market could make a CDO lose value.

Insuring something that is risk-free is a great business to be in, because you never have to pay out. It's literally printing money. Even better for AIG, it was a terrific insurer, and had good relationships with the investment banks like Goldman Sachs and Lehman Brothers who were holding the CDOs. Its assets and track record gave it an AAA credit rating. Even in the middle of 2008 its AA rating – better than Saudi Arabia, China or South Korea – meant that, when it insured CDOs, it didn't have to put up collateral to ensure it could pay the claim.

Anyway, there wouldn't be a claim, because CDOs looked like a one-way bet. The problem was, they looked like a one-way bet because of the methods used to evaluate them.

Credit default swaps (CDSs), as they were called, were cheap compared to the product they insured, because AIG would almost never need to pay out. They had what finance firms call 'high alpha' – low risk, high return. At least, they would if you modelled them over the short or medium term (expecting no, or few, catastrophes) and expected them to be independent (if you pay out for one, the premiums from the others would cover you).

Both are dangerous assumptions. Over the long term, there will be at least one catastrophic event. When that occurs, you may be forced to pay out on many CDSs at the same time. AIG switched from being what we used to call 'as safe as houses' to being a risky bet almost overnight. It's like having a lottery syndicate at work. Every week you are supposed to buy the tickets, but you pocket the cash instead. It's profitable, until your syndicate wins the jackpot.

In 1999, AIGFP had revenues of $737 million. In 2005, they were $3.26 billion. Income for AIGFP was 17.5 per cent of AIG's total income, earned by 0.4 per cent of its employees. Between 2001 and 2008, these employees paid themselves $3.56 billion in bonuses. Writing CDSs, not putting up any collateral, and collecting the fee was making each employee of AIGFP an average of $1 million a year.

Cassano thought, or at least seemed to think, that there was no risk. He sat on an AIG risk management committee, established after 2005. He told a conference of analysts in 2007: 'I think the things that have been put in at our level, and the things that have been put in at the parent level will ensure that there won't be any of those kinds of mistakes again.' For at least the first half of the decade, his assessment was correct. But when sub-prime mortgage holders began to default in high numbers in 2007, and the previously secure CDOs began to take losses that triggered payouts on the

CDSs that his unit had sold, AIGFP began to make heavy losses. For the quarter ending 30 September 2007, those losses were $352 million, and gradually its rating slipped. When its rating dipped below AA in September 2008, because of the way the contracts were written, AIG now had to put up collateral for them – to ensure the counterparties that, if they made a claim, AIG could pay.

AIG had to put up roughly $15 billion, which, not surprisingly, it didn't have on hand.

Crashing the world

On the weekend of 13 and 14 September 2008, the US government had other problems to worry about. It had considered AIG's problem to be manageable. It had already let Bear Stearns fail, and Lehman Brothers was next to go. But AIG was requesting a bail out far bigger than any of them. If AIG failed, the stunned regulators realized, other investment banks, who were its counterparties, would lose billions of dollars. *New York Times* journalist Gretchen Morgenson discovered that Goldman Sachs, considered almost invulnerable to the crisis at that time thanks to its conservative management, had exposure of up to $20 billion if AIG failed. Goldman Sachs disputed the numbers, but we know that $12.9 billion of AIG's bail out funds went directly to it. Cassano, fingered as the culprit, was branded 'the man who crashed the world'.

What is the cost of the AIG bail out? We know very well in the short term, in dollars: about $30 for everyone on the planet. We don't know what kind of value that represents in the long term, in dollars. But the unrepentant behaviour of the employees who believed they had earned their bonuses, and the rush to blame it all on Cassano as a Barings-style 'rogue trader', despite the fact that he had not gone rogue, means that we maybe haven't paid the full price.

AIG didn't fail because it broke the rules. It failed because it conformed to them. They're just ridiculous rules, expectations which shouldn't have applied to AIG, and which overrode the careful, conservative instincts of most within the company.

AIG was part of a culture which needs successful insurance companies to outperform the market just as successful supermarkets or internet retailers do. Which meant that, after more than 70 years in business, AIG had to grab for whatever revenue-boosting strategies it could find. Its early experiments with derivatives were carefully hedged and cleverly written. The employees who created them were fabulously rewarded for writing more of them. When there were no more real CDOs, investment banks manufactured synthetic CDOs, and AIG wrote CDSs for them. As the market appeared to become an automatic teller machine (ATM), its business was eventually exposed as an out-of-control, haphazard mess. Nobody seemed to understand the risk; but even if they did, the AIGFP employees were paid handsomely to invite more of it into the company.

President Obama, explaining the bail out to astonished US citizens on television, said that 'You've got a company, AIG, which used to be just a regular old insurance company. Then they decided – some smart person decided – let's put a hedge fund on top of the insurance company, and let's sell these derivative products to banks all around the world.'[123]

It doesn't sound like something that would make you reach for your Uzi, but it's not just what happened, it's how. The bonuses for failure, and the lack of repentance from employees, rightly make us crazy. What should also make us crazy is that, for banks and insurers, driving forward into high-risk, high-return markets is seen as the natural evolution of their business.

Many successful businesses have been innovative. That doesn't mean that innovation equals success, especially if that innovation comes with unquantified risk. 'We can't control ourselves', John Mack, former chief executive officer (CEO) of Morgan Stanley told Bloomberg Television, when it examined the legacy of AIG in November 2009. 'One of the things that brought down the CEO right before me was that he was not in the markets, he was not taking risks, so the stock went down.'

The money machine
Long Term Capital Management

Economics is constantly renewing and improving its theories as our understanding of the complexity of how we do business with each other, and how we respond to incentives and events, becomes clearer. To the outsider it looks like a branch of mathematics.

The difference is that although the tools of mathematics have been used with great success by economists, those tools arc created in the abstract. Economics deals with the uncertainties of the real world. The real world offers sudden, unexpected events. Modern financial institutions have repeatedly shown that freak events havc devastating consequences. As the size of the gambles they take on increases, the consequences of a freak event become more extreme. And as those banks lend trillions of dollars to each other, when one sneezes, everyone gets a cold.

When it was set up, Long Term Capital Management (LCTM)[124] was the most innovative, cleverest and most radical investment firm we had seen. Backed by Myron Scholes and Robert Merton, the two academics who created the most famous innovations in financial engineering, it seemed to have created perfect money machines.

Yet, a ycar after they won a Nobel prize for their work, LTCM collapsed, and nearly brought down the world's largest investment banks with it. The cause was a single freak event which caused the firm to lose $4.6 billion in four months.

For four years, it appeared that LTCM was the ultimate proof of the concepts that Merton, Scholes and their peers had developed. Founded by John Meriwether, former vice chairman and head of bond trading at Salomon Brothers, it used sophisticated trading models that 'quants' had pioneered in the 1980s and 1990s, taking trading from a dark art to a process where huge, low-risk bets could be made by a PhD and a computer.

Every merchant bank had recruited 'quants' – unusually talented problem solvers with a background in analysis; people who before might have been destined for academia in mathematics or physics. They built models on computers of how the markets worked.

The quants, in turn, were building on a series of innovations created by the work of Merton, Scholes and Fischer Black from the 1970s onwards, which had revolutionized the theory of financial markets. In the 1960s, investing was considered to be about research and knowledge, tied to what companies were producing, selling and creating. Around that time, the first computers were creating a generation of stock market analysts with unprecedented amounts of data.

'Adam Smith', the pseudonymous journalist who was the first to write seriously about modern Wall Street in the 1960s, saw the early advances of computers in his book *The Money Game* in 1967: 'Security analysts used to walk around with a slide rule poking from one pocket... the analysts have taken to using computer words like "input".'

Smith lamented an age in which stock-picking was done by people who could read the movements of a market based on a punched paper tape that scrolled out the news into their computerless offices, and where people made investment decisions based on what companies made or sold.

A new era

Scholes, Merton and others created a string of innovations that would make this view of investment seem rather quaint, and would revolutionize trading along the way. Having become involved with Salomon Brothers, the most innovative derivatives trading firm at the time, the major players decided to set up their own firm with a simple principle: you create a model that finds arbitrage – that is, you find something that is priced too low and buy it, but hedge your bets by selling something that complements it that is priced too high. Whatever happens, you pocket the difference. If the difference is small, you make an enormous investment on both sides.

Meriwether had made billions of dollars for Salomon using this strategy, and when he decided to set up LTCM in 1993, he wanted to refine the principle even further. That led to two decisions: the first was to recruit and pay only the highest level of staff, who could create fantastically complex computer models of a trade, which adjusted continuously to keep taking the tiny amounts caught between buyer and seller. The second was to use huge amounts of borrowed money – leverage, in industry terms – to maximize the return from the trades.

Underpinning this was the assumption that the models created by the two Nobel-winning partners were sound. Which, day to day, they were. Their models made two assumptions: that asset prices, whether they are stocks, bonds, foreign currency or any other investment, move continuously by small amounts. The second is that the markets are liquid: that is, when you want to sell you will find someone to buy by gradually dropping your price until someone takes it; because that's how market prices are created. You may get less than you thought, but someone will, at some price, bite.

LTCM's success from its inception in February 1994 through 1995 and 1996 seemed to reinforce the idea that it had created machines to make money. It was delivering 40 per cent returns every year to its investors making continuous, regular returns, just as the models predicted.

The partners at LTCM weren't naïve: they knew that occasionally a rare event would shift the markets in unexpected ways. They did their own calculations, modelling the effects of earthquakes, wars and business failures, but while the disasters they modelled would knock a hole in their profits, they didn't threaten the firm. Scholes had famously compared LTCM to a vacuum cleaner that picks up discarded nickels: the models were created to ensure that LTCM was as close to being a one-way bet as possible.

Risk and reward

For external consumption it also used the value-at-risk (VAR) model to calculate the risk of a disaster, which adds up the value of all its trades, models the effect of unusual deviations in the market price of assets, and gives a simple figure for how much the fund would lose, as a maximum, 19 days out of 20. It's still a standard measure of risk for financial services companies.

VAR has been exposed more recently as a poor measure of risk management; while few financial institutions rely on it, the easy-to-understand figures it produces undoubtedly give the board a misleading picture of what might happen: because the 19 days aren't as important as the 20th. If there is the possibility of a catastrophic failure on one of the days when the bank breaches its limits, then VAR – or any in-house risk measurement method – might not be as reassuring as it seems.

Richard Bennett, the managing director at Razor Risk, provides risk management products that use a 'Monte Carlo' simulation to model every possible combination of markets, trends and behaviour. If one, any one, causes the bank to fail, it's not invulnerable. He says that many institutions, like LTCM, still convince themselves that they cannot fail – especially when they are making large returns:

I say, don't just look at the five years before the crisis. Because their risk systems are older than the products, many banks have great difficulty putting new types of trade into their risk management systems. They can't incorporate all the data. They make large assumptions with respect to the mathematical foundations. And they never fully understand the risks they run when they are scaled to the whole business.

By 1998, encouraged by its risk modelling, LTCM (already borrowing more than 30 times its equity base) was looking to increase the amount of leverage over time. No one considered this to be a problem, because the way it invested ensured that a loss in one area would be directly compensated by a profit in another. The fund had even returned $2.7 billion of investors' money in 1997, because it didn't need it to prop up positions that amounted to approximately $1.25 trillion.

LTCM had no problem borrowing the money from investment banks, because it was brilliant. The firm had equity of $4.72 billion and had borrowed more than $124.5 billion.

Broken models

One of the wonders of hedging is that many of those $1.25 trillion positions effectively cancelled each other out: if you borrow £5 from your brother at 5 per cent and lend £5 to your sister at 10 per cent, you have positions of £10, but a guaranteed profit. If something goes wrong, you pay your brother with a fiver and change from your wallet. If you want to make a bigger profit, and you borrow £500 million from your brother, lend the same to your sister, she puts it into a bank in Moscow and the Russian government says she can't get it back for another month, you will need to find the £500 million somewhere else when your brother wants his money back. If your family loses confidence in your ability to pay, they're not going to lend you money, and they're all going to want their £500 million back at the same time.

This, simplified massively, is what happened to LTCM. In August 1998, it had massive investments in the Russian rouble. The unexpected event that its risk calculations did not predict was that the Russian government devalued the rouble and blocked investors from getting out of their dollar-to-rouble contracts for one month. As rumours spread that LTCM was suffering, its competitors refused to lend it support. They had no idea whether they would see their money back.

The two things that broke the models of Merton and Scholes happened: some of their complicated assets became impossible to price, while others were illiquid, and wouldn't sell at any price. LTCM was suddenly making massive bets without control. Previously the business had been about hedging everything it did: creating a system of trades where, if one price went down, another went up, and a nickel would be squeezed out whatever happened. When the markets behaved unpredictably, the models which had created these $1.25 trillion positions proved impossible to dismantle, and simply became machines for losing money, instead of making it. In the panic, LTCM traders had abandoned their discipline as the fund attempted to recoup value and had made one-way, unhedged, bets.

Panicked clients, seeing what was happening, wanted their cash back. By 25 September, LTCM had just $400 million in capital. With assets of still more than $100 billion, this translated to an effective leverage ratio of more than 250:1. With other options, the Federal Reserve Bank of New York organized an emergency bail out of a firm that few people outside the financial markets even knew existed. Major creditors provided $3.625 billion to avoid a wider collapse in the financial markets: LTCM's positions were so huge that if it had failed suddenly, the world's financial markets might have seized up. A consortium of investors put together $400 million to take the positions from LTCM and slowly dismantle them. The fund covered its debts, and was closed in early 2000, taking with it the life savings of its partners, who together had invested $1.9 billion in LTCM. It also took the savings, and some of the reputation, of the two Nobel laureates who were partners in the firm.

We are more aware of the possibilities of sudden catastrophic events, not least because the trader Nassim Nicholas Taleb has popularized the discussion in his book *The Black Swan*.[125] Yet Bennett laments that some of the banks he speaks to still believe in the invulnerability of their thinking; they look at the 19 days that they will operate inside their limits, not the 20th day when they breach them. One major bank, he says, responded to its losses in the financial crisis by saying that its budgets had been cut: so it couldn't afford to upgrade its risk management systems.

Myron Scholes, writing in the *American Economic Review* in May 2000, had changed his opinion of the invulnerability of hedge funds like LTCM. 'Planning for crises is more important than VAR analysis', he warned. He should know.

Paying the price *Letsbuyit.com*

Innovation around a simple idea works well. But there comes a time in every company's life when it needs, according to conventional management wisdom, a BHAG – a Big Hairy Audacious Goal. So while Bill Gates wanted to put a computer on every desk, his spiritual successors at dot-com start-up Letsbuyit. com – at one time Europe's largest e-commerce site in terms of customer and visitor numbers – wanted to put a Christmas tree in every house.

The BHAG concept was created by James Collins and Jerry Porras in a 1996 article called 'Building Your Company's Vision'. Collins and Porras have credibility: they developed the concept further in the management bible *Built to Last*. The BHAG goes beyond mere operational goals and creates a vision that stretches years into the future. It can motivate staff and give their work a purpose beyond the day to day.

This is, however, seen through the eyes of companies that created BHAGs and made a success of them. By their nature they are difficult, and that success would mean the failure of competitors. It requires learning new skills, and testing your organization to the limit.

So it's not surprising that most don't make it. For the CEO this can be a learning experience, or the failure which makes them stronger. For the staff it's redundancy and a colossal waste of time. Afterwards we shake our heads and say, 'What were they thinking?'

Truth is, very often they were thinking the same as us: it's crazy, but it might just work. This was the philosophy that underpinned much of the dot-com boom. It even created a website where insiders posted tips of the horrible failure of their companies, called F*ckedCompany.com. It was, for a time, funny and horrible: eRegister.com, and its 'innovative registration solutions' ($5 million funding for a website that helped you register for things), Impresse, which allowed people to shop around for cheap printing using the internet ($90 million funding), or Refer.com, which let you recommend someone, and when they got hired, you got $1,000. Though why anyone who didn't know you would hire someone because you said they were good was never explained.

Those ideas, however, were clearly idiotic. Not so with Letsbuyit.com. Which, we must point out, is not today's Letsbuyit.com. We're talking about version 1, which was created in an altogether different age.

The company was set up in Sweden in 1999 as a modern incarnation of the co-operative movement that flourished in the 19th century. The co-ops were owned by their members, who banded together to get better prices on the essentials that they needed to live. Profits were shared among members.

Letsbuyit.com took this to the internet. It offered a choice of consumer goods, and you registered to buy. The more people who clubbed together, the lower the price. The company negotiated bulk discounts with suppliers, and handled the shipping.

This produced a marginal benefit for some products (frankly, not that much when you consider that as soon as major suppliers went online, they had already achieved the bulk discount, and so could match the price without the risk or the wait). But Letsbuyit.com saw its future as more than just a supplier of CD players and inkjet printers: it wanted to be the method by which we got best prices on everything. It would be the consumer champion.

Supported by investment capital and TV advertising, it had good numbers: 80,000 products, 100,000 visitors a day, sites in 11 countries within one year of launch; but it needed to reach ordinary people, most of whom in 2000 were suspicious of the internet, and internet-based shopping in particular.

A sourcing issue

And so it was that in November 1999, for its UK launch, Letsbuyit.com had a wonderful idea. It would deliver Christmas trees to us all. If 499 people signed up for a £20 Christmas tree, the price would be discounted by £13. Helped by an excited and approving press, many thousands ordered trees. This was the internet revolution marketed in a way that ordinary families and people without MBAs could understand.

One problem: because of its business model, Letsbuyit.com didn't have any actual trees. It might also have occurred that, even at the most competitive rates imaginable, sourcing, importing, selling and delivering a seasonal product wasn't going to be either easy or profitable, especially for a company that had been in business for less than 12 months.

And so the excited acclaim was matched by amused derision when consumers received their Christmas trees. In January 2000.

Big, hairy, audacious and, it seems, impossible. It dented their popularity, but not, according to my notes, their confidence. In early 2000 I interviewed

John Palmer, who was running the UK operation. 'We're in 14 markets today, by the end of the year we want to be in 25', he told me. 'Co-buying is mainstream. It's not an eccentric niche. When we sell, we sell in quantity... We haven't gone crazy, and we have enough money left to keep expanding. We have half a million members: 30 per cent purchase again, and they will come back on average four times.'

Maeve Garrety, who at the time was head of the future consumer practice at management consultancy DeCipher, which helped plan retail strategies for Tesco, among others, was bowled over, despite the unfortunate tree business. 'We think it's a great concept, it builds on the fundamental strength of the net, and that's community... Letsbuyit.com is Virginesque – it might not have a huge amount of share, but it's shaking up the market already. It will change people's perception of the internet.'

But enthusiasm for this perception-changing company had almost run out. Later in 2000, Letsbuyit.com managed to go public, floating shares on the German Neuer Markt in July at the third attempt. Its July flotation raised €66 million, less than half of what it hoped for. It didn't get a chance to correct the mistake: by December 2000 the site had suspended trading and cancelled Christmas orders, and was apparently looking for another €80 million to keep going; €80 million which never arrived. A month later the company's trustees were describing the management as 'deplorable', and the management were challenging the forced bankruptcy in court.[126]

The Kimpire

It gets odder after this, because at least one large person decided the revolution was not over: after several potential investors looked at the books and decided not to get involved, attempts to salvage the company were led by 23-stone ex-hacker and entrepreneur Kim Schmitz, also known as 'Kimble', who paid €2.5 million as part of a group of investors to save the company in January 2001. 'The rules in my world are not the rules of the old economy. This is the cyber age, which allows the Kimpire to grow fast, cost efficiently and without any limits. No bureaucracy, paragraphs or borders can slow down the Kimpire. Our brains and the Internet, that's all we need to be successful', he once posted on his website. Brains, the internet and something else: he was later found guilty by a Munich court of insider trading in shares in the company, and given a 20-month suspended sentence and a fine.[127]

Without the support of the Kimpire the company still managed to avoid bankruptcy, but only by changing its business model – not least because it had simultaneously lost the confidence of consumers and suppliers. And without them, there wasn't really much left. The name survives; the BHAG of a global consumer co-operative does not. Today if you go to http://www. letsbuyit.com you will find a completely unrelated but standard price comparison website. On which, of course, you can find the best price for a Christmas tree – which will be delivered to you before Christmas.

The next level *Digiscents*

When Jonathan Seidenfeld joined Digiscents ('the pioneer of digital scent technology') as senior director of business development, games and entertainment, he told the press that 'Just as the PlayStation revolutionized interactive games, the iSmell will take games to the next level of immersion and realism.'[128]

We have to accept that in any bubble there will be many bad companies created. Many of the failures were simply not innovative enough: offering ways to sell the same products which were not as convenient, cheap or entertaining as the ways we already had – a flaw not immediately obvious to the (admittedly substantial) number of people who were just in love with the technology. In that case, the enthusiasm of the entrepreneurs was markedly at odds with the product or service they were showing us.

But some people contributed at the other end of the scale, coming up with ideas that were so ridiculously creative that most people assumed they were simply a silly joke. That's the problem with amazingly bright people: they need people who are bright in more ordinary ways to tell them when they are wasting their time. What they sometimes don't need is $20 million in funding.

The creative people of whom I speak are Dexster Smith and Joel Bellenson, who had contributed hugely to the public good with a software company called Double Twist, about which nothing bad can be said. In 1999 Double Twist earned its founders great admiration, and rightly so: it was the first to annotate the human genome, which is an intellectual achievement that, in the future, will probably have them remembered in the same way as we remember the Victorians who created the railways, or discovered how to transmit electricity.

Smith and Bellenson also proved their worth as citizens, because they made the results available to academics for free. At the same time, a company called Celera was engaged on the same project. It intended to protect its research, which would have been a great advantage for Celera, but arguably not so excellent for the rest of the human race.

For this, alone, they deserve not to be made fun of. Except, that is, for what they did next.

A bad smell

Their 1999 innovation shows how clever people can really produce a stink: this was iSmell. iSmell's idea was to create something that was a bit like an inkjet printer for the nose. The printer contained 128 different scented oils, and when you downloaded a file, opened an e-mail or visited a web page, it would combine the oils to generate the appropriate smell for the occasion, depending on code that the developer had put into the web page.

Though it sounds like a spoof, it did exist. One of my colleagues saw it in action. The product, thankfully, never went beyond prototype, but it still managed to cause a stink. It had burned through all its $20 million funding by the time the company shut down in 2001.

But how could these young geniuses know it was a stink bomb of an innovation? Perhaps by wondering if this innovation hadn't already caused general mirth. If they had looked back 40 years, before either of them was born, they would have found records of Smell-O-vision and AromaRama, two competing technologies to make movie theatres smell like the films they were showing. The system was quite similar in concept, but instead of a computer printer, the movie theatres used pipes to waft the scent to the audience. It wasn't hugely successful. The trouble is that smells tend to hang around, so five minutes after you've smelt the roses, they're still lingering while you watch the roller-coaster riders plunging to their deaths.

Also, it's quite hard to get people excited about the opportunity to smell things, if they don't know what the smell's going to be. 'First they moved! Then they talked! Now they smell!' was the advertising copy for the moviegoers, which inexplicably didn't find a mass market.

Digiscents might have taken the hint: soon after it was founded, Smell-O-Vision was voted one of the 100 worst ideas of the 20th century by *Time Magazine*. But there was something in the air in 1999 which made pointless innovations like this seem possible. As the advertising copy for Smell-O-Vision encouraged us to do 40 years earlier, you had to 'Breathe It to Believe it'.

One of the business ideas for the iSmell was to get funding from perfumiers. But these companies earn big money because it's hard to mix a smell that smells right. It's unlikely they'd trust a smell-printer-thingy. And, outside their meeting rooms, they might have noticed that nobody sits in front of a computer thinking: 'I wonder what that smells like?'

Like Smell-O-Rama, iSmell will always be an award-winner: *PC Magazine*, the geek bible, voted it one of the 25 worst tech ideas of all time. Considering how much competition there was during this era, this accolade was quite hard to get. *PC Magazine* described the product: 'a shark-fin-shaped gizmo that plugged into your PC's USB port and wafted appropriate scents as you surfed smell-enabled Web sites'.

Someone who worked for the company should have taken the guys to one side and told them: 'you're brilliant, and creative, and wonderful human beings. For God's sake stop talking to the press about this.' But, to do that, they would have needed to have doubted the genius of a box on your desk that made the room smell every time you went on the internet. It seems that Digiscents had recruited well, and found the small group of people in the world who actually thought this was a good idea.

Chad Dickerson, an industry veteran and at the time the chief technology officer (CTO) of the Infoworld Media Group, recalls a meeting[129] with the developers of the iSmell in which they innovated a new buzzword: 'a person on their end of the table uttered a line with a completely straight face that pretty much encapsulated the simultaneous seriousness and insanity of the dotcom era: "We're building a portal of digital smells – a snortal".'

Bigger than the internet *Segway*

There's a rule of thumb in the newspaper business which helps you to spot hyperbole.[130] When you see a headline which has a question mark at the end of it, just try saying 'No' in your head when you read it.

Try it: 'Will a scooter, no matter how cool it may be, really revolutionize the world?' asked *Wired* magazine in January 2001. See?

Wired was speculating about the first exciting rush of gossip based on the leak that Dean Kamen, an entrepreneur and inventor, had a prototype for a product codenamed 'ginger'.[131]

You might still not have heard of Kamen, but he was, still is, and probably always will be a talented, successful and resourceful inventor, who is driven by the idea that he can use great ideas to change the world. Kamen was never destined for middle management.

After dropping out of college he created – among other things – the iBot wheelchair, a technological marvel which balanced using sensors and could climb stairs.

'Don't tell me it's impossible,' he told *Esquire Magazine* in 2008, 'tell me you can't do it.' He was friends with Bill Clinton. He lived in a hexagonal house. What, the gossip asked, would he come up with next?

A few sensible people pointed out that, given the technology he created for the iBot, which seems to balance itself almost in mid-air, a simple transportation device using similar technology was a next step. Others pointed out that he had already, ahem, built a prototype: 'Dean's two-wheel balancing device is really cool', Dr Wise Young at Rutgers University told *Wired*. 'It zooms around like lightning just by standing on it and leaning forward or backwards.' That was, we could agree, really cool.

But such down-to-earth speculation somehow wasn't enough: Ginger started to attract speculation that it wouldn't change personal transportation, it would change the world. Maybe we were excited by his reputation. Maybe we were more comfortable with that sort of thing, after the success of a few internet companies which really did look like they would change the world – even if most of them have really just changed the way we shop. Maybe it was because the fizz had gone out of dot-com, and we were looking for a new type of genius.

And in the absence of other information, we preferred the idea that someone was going to change the world to the idea that he'd built a scooter. Journalists, when speculating, never failed to mention the first two comments from the first wire report on Ginger: 'Amazon.com CEO Jeff Bezos says it's a "product so revolutionary, you'll have no problem selling it." Apple Computer CEO Steve Jobs says it will change the ways cities are designed.'

A new world

It's hard to fit a scooter into the concept of world-changingness, no matter how much coffee you've had, so *Wired* upped the speculation:

> Kamen has a patent, issued last year, that outlines a design for a Stirling engine. This alternative power source would fit better with the descriptions offered by people who claim to have seen the device, such as 3Com's Bob Metcalfe, who described IT as 'almost as big as cold fusion would have been.'... a commercially viable Stirling engine would be a non-polluting, cheap power source that could completely change the dynamics of the dependency upon the Middle East's oil producing regions and cause fuel prices to tumble. It could, scientists say, launch a new world.

Hang on, Bob Metcalfe had said that it was almost as big as cold fusion?

Here's the problem with leaks: with 24-hour media outlets, no news is simply not good enough. As no news filtered through about Ginger during 2001, and magazines and newspapers that had expanded their technology sections massively to make room for all the dot-com successes that had turned to failures looked for a new hero, Ginger looked the best bet.

Between leak and launch there were around 350 articles published to gossip about the invention. Two-thirds of them recycled the comment attributed to Jobs, who – it later transpired – had actually told the inventor that the design 'sucked'. What a buzzkill. Around the same proportion recycled Bezos' attributed opinion on its revolutionaryness. Another 50 or so enthusiastically carried the reported opinion of the venture capitalist John Doerr, who had set up funding of $38 million for the product, that Ginger would maybe be bigger than the internet, and would be the fastest outfit in history to reach $1 billion in sales. Few mentioned that he was basically advertising a product that he had paid for. It was simply too exciting.

On 3 December 2001 the device was revealed, not at a trade show, but on *Good Morning America*: the revolutionary product that would change cities and rival unlimited power was: the Segway scooter.

It turned out that the first guess that *Wired* made was correct, and the exaggerated speculation afterwards was all a feverish dream. When the fever broke, you could almost hear millions of households saying, 'That's it? A scooter?'

The product, with which you are probably now familiar – today they are used to ferry tubby tourists around outdoor experiences or in shopping malls – operated for two hours, could travel 17 miles, and could reach 17 miles per hour. It cost around $3,000. A custom-built factory could create 40,000 Segways a month, including specially designed industrial and military versions.

The hype around Segway filled a gap for disappointed technology enthusiasts. Until the dot-com boom, technology was really interesting only to a small group of enthusiasts. People who stayed at home to program their computer, or got excited about personal electronics, were amusing. For two years, it was the focus of our excitement: we were building the new world. Ginger was the next great hope for a better society after we discovered that the dot-com boom wasn't all it seemed.

Details, details

That meant that we were prepared to overlook some of the more important problems. There was nowhere to park them. Where would you use them? Pavements, especially in car-crazy US suburbs, were often too small to avoid knocking pedestrians over. Segways were slow enough to be dangerous on a road. Would people use them when it rained? Did you need to wear a helmet? It would have taken a generation and billions of dollars to rebuild US cities – many of which had grown by building suburbs many miles outside the city limits, with only the freeway to provide access to the places where people could work. All of which made it unlikely that the Segway would be 'to the car what the car was to the horse and buggy', as Kamen had told *Time* Magazine.[132]

Let's not also forget that not everyone likes a revolution. Had it been an initial success, the backlash from the auto industry would have been massive. In technology – the home territory of Bezos and Jobs and Metcalfe – if a product looks like stealing your business, you get engineers to reverse engineer it as soon as possible so that you can copy it. This may or may not work, but it creates projects to produce lookalikes, and competition that creates better versions of the same product. Think of genuinely revolutionary technologies, such as the mobile phone. It's rarely like that when it comes to personal transportation. The auto business has, instead, a variety of blocking tactics: it has skilled lobbyists in Washington and a lot of lawyers, and there was a $3 billion US business at stake.

But no panic measures were necessary. The bubble of excitement popped as soon as we were faced with the product. In 2003 Segway sold just 6,000 units. A recall in September 2006 forced the company to reveal that it had, at that time, approximately 23,500 users. *Time Magazine*, once the cheerleader for the Segway, speculated that the product recall wasn't a reputational disaster for Segway – because so few people knew it existed, the Segway didn't have a reputation to lose.

In December 2001 Michael Schmertzler from Credit Suisse First Boston, Segway's other major financial backer, told *Time* that 'this is about more than money for Dean. Pardon the cliche, but he really does want to change the world.' In 2010, Segway had not yet changed the world: the company was sold to a UK-based group of businesspeople. It's still illegal to ride one in the UK: South Yorkshire Police charged 51-year-old Phillip Coates for riding one on Barnsley's pavements, under the 1835 Highways Act.

Kamen is still a creative genius. In 2009, he designed a new soft drink vending machine for Coca Cola, which he believes may lead to spin-off technologies to provide safe water in the developing world. Maybe it's not his fault that the Segway hype got so out of hand; but it's the failure that he may ultimately be remembered for.

When Segway was bought by its British investors, in eight years the company had sold 'over 50,000' Segways – just over one month's projected production for Kamen's giant factory.

The invisible hand

On 19 February 2009, US Network CNBC on-air editor Rick Santelli was loud, even by his standards. Booming away from the floor of the Chicago Mercantile Exchange (CME), he was surrounded by traders, all of whom seemed to share his disgust at the US government's attempt to bail out homeowners who were close to foreclosure. 'The government is promoting bad behaviour', he shouted on live TV. 'Have a referendum to see if we really want to subsidize the losers' mortgages... The founding fathers: What we're doing in this country now is making them roll over in their graves.'

Egged on by the anchors in the studio, who joked that he should 'do that one more time, get the mob behind you', Santelli told us that the lesson of the financial crisis was that 'You can't buy your way into prosperity.' Of course, he didn't mean that no one could buy their way into prosperity. That's what the companies that CNBC swoons over had been doing, increasingly, for decades. That's what 'leverage' is, and will always be: buying your way into prosperity using someone else's money. If you fail, they don't get it back.

What Santelli meant was that it was OK for successful people and firms to buy their way into prosperity. His opinion was loudly echoed by the traders on the floor of the CME, who hooted along in approval of what was later dubbed by newspapers 'the rant of the year'.

American entrepreneurs built an economy from almost nothing at the beginning of the 19th century to the largest in the world in less than 100 years. In the 19th century Chicago, where Santelli stood, was more a village than a city.

If Santelli had spent less time shouting to the mob and more time actually reading what the founding fathers wrote, he'd find a different message. The early years of the United States produced a large number of books designed to help the readers become successful. One of the most popular was *The Way to Wealth* written by Benjamin Franklin. 'The second vice is lying, the first is running in debt. And again to the same purpose, lying rides upon debt's back,' he writes in *The Way to Wealth*, 'rather go to bed supperless than rise in debt.'

Not many of the banks and businesses that Santelli defends went to bed supperless, and debt made liars out of many of them. Undoubtedly more than we know.

The business of success is more profitable, especially for the management, than it has ever been. But increasingly it's a business that involves unquantifiable risk and unethical or borderline-ethical accounting.

The idea of success that the founding fathers espoused wasn't simply the ability to get rich. It offered the end product as the prize for a life lived in pursuit of a dream which had meaning. They stressed hard work and ethical behaviour, the ability to create wealth that would lift your family and children out of poverty forever, acquired over a lifetime of application.

Franklin might have recognized, but certainly wouldn't have approved of, the massaged numbers that ultimately broke Enron and WorldCom; the sense of entitlement that caused GM to coast to a stop; the slash-and-burn short-termism of Al Dunlap; the opaque gambling practised by Lehman Brothers or Long Term Capital Management; or the crazy speculation that almost bankrupted Iceland.

Innovation corrupted

If you let people succeed and others fail, and we live in something that roughly approximates a meritocracy, so that good things succeed and bad things fail, our lives improve. Being surrounded by stuff that works is better than going back to the 1970s. Believe me, I know. I lived in the 1970s for 10 years.

If you let failures fail, then the wealth created by successes can be used to make them bigger or more efficient, because they seem to know what they are doing. Wealth is given as a reward to the people who helped create it, or used so that those people can walk the earth and make other companies successful. This much is good, as long as it works that way.

This narrative, we are led to believe, written by Adam Smith's 'invisible hand', show the economic processes which produce the most efficient outcomes. Joseph Stiglitz, Nobel prize-winning economist and a fierce critic of the conduct of business in the developed world, thinks that the meritocracy has been corrupted: 'One thing economists agree on: incentives matter. In recent history, [management] had the incentive to be short sighted, to take excessive risk. A new generation grew up that came to believe that markets were always efficient. In reality, the reason that the invisible hand seemed invisible was that it wasn't there.'

The modern examples in this book show that we don't seem any better than the Tulip brokers of the Netherlands or the investors in the South Sea bubble at eliminating boom-and-bust or resisting get-rich-quick schemes, or standing up to bullies when they're wrong. We still habitually credit powerful people with intelligence when all the evidence is to the contrary, and refuse to listen to contrarians until it's too late. We follow the herd and believe the conventional wisdom. We trust optimism more than analysis if the analysis is pessimistic.

We trust industries to regulate themselves while incentivizing them to take risks, and nothing short of a meltdown leads to a suggestion that we could, perhaps, do something differently. Then we let them talk us out of it. The next time there's a bust, we act like it's a surprise, and decide that something must be done.

Einstein's definition of madness was doing the same thing over and over, and expecting a different result. Cars will always crash; but more crash if you get the drivers drunk and tell them to drive as fast as possible.

A Mexican soap opera

Big business is about strategy and rationality, but that's not why we are fascinated by it. It's also about prejudice, fashion and emotion. The unpredictable twists, the heroes corrupted by greed or ambition, the avenging accountants, the man whose time has come, the visionaries whose dreams are dashed, all make the history of business failure into a sort of Mexican soap opera.

Men like John Law and Clarence Hatry have always captured the public imagination, but today's business leaders have more news coverage and more melodramatic adulation than ever. We solicit their views not just on the performance of their own companies, but on government policy, the law, ethics, morality. We are more familiar with the chief executives of supermarkets than with government ministers or religious leaders. Business has become a battle of Big Ideas, but not always good ideas.

Business books sell strategy as if, to get to Paradise, we just need to follow a set of instructions. Problem is, which religion do we follow? Do we invite dissent (a good idea), or do we have a 'No a**hole rule' (another good idea)? Do we restlessly innovate, or do we stick to our core competency? Do we cut costs or generate sales?

When a company succeeds, having followed this year's management fashion, do we conclude that those ideas made it successful? Possibly, but as Machiavelli tells us in *The Prince*: only at that time, only in those conditions, only that company.

The trouble with soaps is that the characters never develop. It's just a set of actions and reactions, heroes and villains, winners and losers. If we simply reflate the bubble and start again, we're risking far worse failures in the future: bigger frauds, crazier CEOs, more reckless gambles. As John Mack, the former CEO of Morgan Stanley, said: We cannot control ourselves.

We even manipulate the storyline, often for the direct financial benefit of the managers involved, by stretching the boundaries of accountancy once a quarter. It's extremely precise, but that doesn't make it accurate.

We don't mind as much as we should. We're captured by the excitement of the bullsh*t ideology that says all we need to do is to leave the running of business to successful businesses, and we'll all be better off. It never worked that way, and it never will.

Full disclosure

It's important to those who want to retain their influence over the political process and their personal wealth that we feel super-happy about business. We spend most of our waking lives trying to create success at work, and most of the rest shopping for the things that other people make when they're at work, even if we don't really need them. We need to feel good about borrowing money to pay for those things that we don't really need. Now we also need to be contented by the thought that we've bailed out the companies who went bust because they wanted to borrow money to buy things too.

We also need to be entertained by commerce, like restless children. We fit the stories of successful companies to the storybooks of how good triumphs over evil, how great men change history, or how the wilderness was tamed.

Our narrative falls apart when success abruptly turns to failure, because we have awarded attributes to the CEOs that we wish for ourselves. Often we conclude that the good things were down to our heroes, and the bad things can hardly be their fault. They are only too happy to confirm this view. We still marvel at their bonuses, their private jets, their houses, their antique commodes. We are half disgusted, half turned on.

Compared to anaemic politicians and smaller-than-life film stars, business is fun to watch. Our childish excitement suits the people who profit from booms and seek to dodge the impact of the bust.

One of the stranger outcomes of Enron's journey from fit to bust: in August 2002, *Playboy* printed one of its most popular pictorials ever, featuring ex-employees of Enron – whose collapse nine months earlier had destroyed $1.2 billion of retirement funds for its former employees. 'Though the dream dried up for the bankrupt energy firm Enron, 10 of its employees decided to shed, not shred, for *Playboy*,' it explained, jauntily. 'Too bad Enron execs didn't learn the same lesson that when it comes to assets, full disclosure is the way to go.'

The 10 Women of Enron, draped over office desks or flashing perkily outside their former headquarters, managed to do something that our parents wouldn't have believed was possible. They made redundancy erotic.

Sources and Notes

Chapter One

1 The list of brands that will disappear is at http://24/7wallst. com/2010/06/15/247-wall-st-ten-brands-that-will-disappear-in-2011/.

2 *Fast Company*'s article on *Built to Last* is at http://www.fastcompany.com/ magazine/88/built-to-last.html.

3 The Macmillan quotation can't be substantiated, and so it has joined the list of quotations that might never have been spoken, but probably was at some point. See Robert Harris for more detail: http://www.telegraph.co.uk/ comment/personal-view/3577416/As-Macmillan-never-said-thats-enough-quotations.html.

4 D'Aveni's quote is from the *Fast Company* article, above.

5 'Management Advice: Which 90% is Crap?' Bob Sutton, 2006. Download from Change This: http://changethis.com/manifesto/show/23.90PercentCrap.

6 You can download Machiavelli's *The Prince* for free from Project Gutenberg among other sources: http://www.gutenberg.org/etext/1232.

Chapter Two

Bernard Madoff

7 The news coverage of the Madoff story tracks the unfolding astonishment of those who were defrauded. The *Financial Times* collects its coverage in one archive: http://www.ft.com/indepth/madoff-scandal.

8 Quotes used in this section from the BBC documentary *Madoff: The $65 billion swindle*, first broadcast 29 June 2009

9 'SEC censured after missed opportunities over Madoff', *FT*, 7 September 2009

10 Watch the Markopolos testimony here: http://www.youtube.com/ watch?v=uw_Tgu0txS0.

WorldCom

11 For analysis of the fraud, the primary source is the SEC Report Of Investigation By The Special Investigative Committee Of The Board Of Directors Of Worldcom, Inc., Dennis R Beresford, Nicholas deB Katzenbach

and C B Rogers, Jr, 2003. Download it here: http://www.sec.gov/Archives/edgar/data/723527/000093176303001862/dex991.htm.

12   The quotes in this section are mainly taken from Robert S Kaplan and David Kiron, *Accounting Fraud at WorldCom* (Harvard Business School, 2007) and *What went wrong at WorldCom?* (Wharton Business School, 2002).

13   Senator Stevens actually said that 'The Internet is not something that you just dump something on. It's not a big truck. It's a series of tubes', during a debate on 28 June 2006. At this point he was in charge of regulating the internet, so it's easy to understand why companies like WorldCom were not scared of the US government.

Enron

14   Skilling was convicted on 25 May 2006.

15   You can watch Enron's visionary advertising here: http://www.rtmark.com/enron/.

16   A good backgrounder to this is Mimi Swartz and Sherron Watkins, *Power Failure: The inside story of the collapse of Enron* (Doubleday, 2003).

17   This is explained excellently in Bethany McLean and Peter Elkind, *Smartest Guys in the Room: The amazing rise and scandalous fall of Enron* (Portfolio, 2003) – or, if you prefer, the documentary of the same name.

18   Prof. Salter published his research in 2008 in *Innovation Corrupted: The origins and legacy of Enron's collapse* (Harvard University Press). He is interviewed about the book here: http://hbswk.hbs.edu/item/5950.html.

The numbers game

19   Joseph Stiglitz, *The Roaring Nineties* (W.W. Norton, 2003)

20   http://www.darden.virginia.edu/corporate-ethics/

21   Full report here: news.findlaw.com/wp/docs/enron/specinv020102rpt1.pdf.

Chapter Three

22   'The man with the trillion dollar price on his head', *Sunday Times*, 17 May 2009

Northern Rock

23   *Daily Telegraph*, 16 September 2007

24   The full report is here (warning: it's 181 pages long): http://www.parliament.the-stationery-office.com/pa/cm200708/cmselect/cmtreasy/56/5602.htm.

25   The Nationwide House Price Index is at http://www.nationwide.co.uk/hpi/.

26 In 2009 Global Futures and Foresight researched the UK's 'vintage years' for Penfold's winery: low crime, high employment and high home ownership were factors. 'The two highest-scoring Penfold's Vintage Years were in the middle of the noughties boom, 2004 and 2003', it concluded. http://www. thegff.com/Articles/215124/Global_Futures_and/Reports/Penfolds_Vintage_ Years/Penfolds_Vintage_Years.aspx

27 Self-cert mortgages could skew market: http://news.bbc.co.uk/1/hi/ business/3478635.stm. The quotes that follow are from the same source.

28 'Lender offers over 7.5 times income to mortgage borrowers', *Daily Mail*, 27 October 2006

29 View King's testimony to the Treasury Select Committee after the crisis had concluded: http://bbc.in/dTBsXt.

30 http://www.independent.co.uk/news/business/analysis-and-features/was-the-last-fall-in-house-prices-just-a-warning-2034677.html

Barings Bank

31 Barings' star employee, Nick Leeson, is now an after-dinner speaker. Read his account of the collapse: Nick Leeson and Edward Whitley, *Rogue Trader: How I brought down Barings Bank and shook the financial world* (Sphere, 1996). Or visit his website: http://www.nickleeson.com/. Or, if you must, watch the film of the book.

32 Barings is undoubtedly the inspiration for Adam Haslett's plausible novel *Union Atlantic*, published in 2010 by Random House. Haslett's novel, though, focuses not on the rogue trader, but on his boss. In the fictional treatment, the boss is complicit in cutting corners and hiding data, but doesn't appreciate the full scale of the disaster until it is too late.

33 He was Prime Minister of France at the time.

34 Satyajit Das, *Traders, Guns and Money* (Prentice Hall, 2006).

35 *Report Of The Board Of Banking Supervision Inquiry Into The Circumstances Of The Collapse Of Barings*. http://www.numa.com/ref/ barings/bar00.htm

36 Quoted in *Rogue Trader*.

37 A balanced review of the events, which focuses on the structures rather than the personalities, is *The Barings Collapse*, published by the International Institute for Management in 1995.

The Mississippi Company

38 http://www.pierre-marteau.com/editions/1709-cambio-mercatorio.html

39 *The Crayon Papers*, Washington Irving, 1819

40 An entertaining and vivid version of this story is in *Extraordinary Popular Delusions and the Madness of Crowds*, published by Charles Mackay in 1841, and reprinted constantly since. Mackay defends Law, and heaps almost all the blame on the dastardly French.

Leeds United plc

41 Peter Ridsdale's account of the fall of Leeds United was published as *United We Fall: Boardroom truths about the beautiful game* (Macmillan, 2007), which was disputed by some of the other characters in the story. Notably, David O'Leary called him 'deranged' in an interview with the *Daily Mail*.

42 Nick Hornby, *Fever Pitch* (Gollancz, 1992)

43 The clearest investigation into how Leeds was financed, and the most dispassionate one, is the article 'Money to burn' by Brian Cathcart in the *Observer*, 7 March 2004.

44 Phil Rostron, *Leeds United: Trial and Tribulations* (Mainstream Publishing, 2004)

45 'Mugged and violated, Portsmouth fans must be granted full investigation', *The Guardian*, 28 February 2010

Upselling the dream

46 Among the brands that do this: Proctor & Gamble hired 600,000 mothers in the United States to spread the word about its products. Read more in *Obsessive Branding Disorder* by Lucas Conley (PublicAffairs Books, 2008).

47 15 March 2009

48 'Office staff warned of confrontation as City braces for mass G20 protests', *The Guardian*, 22 March 2009

49 *The Onion* often seems to be a more reliable news source than the newspapers it spoofs: http://www.theonion.com/articles/nation-ready-to-be-lied-to-about-economy-again,2717/.

50 'Who Lobbies for the Rest of Us?' http://bit.ly/hrihpW

51 'The Media-Lobbying complex', *The Nation*, 11 February 2010

52 http://www.imf.org/external/pubs/ft/wp/2009/wp09287.pdf

Chapter Four

53 'Are CEOs and celebrities worth the big bucks?', ABC News, 15 January 2009

54 Gates told *Playboy Magazine* in 1994 that 'I'm in the same traffic as everybody else. I'm in the same airplane delay as everybody else. I sit in the same coach seat as everybody else.' Later in the interview he added that, when it comes to stories told about him, 'There are elements of truth in all mythology, along with a good dose of exaggeration that I have not contributed to.' If you've flown with him in economy class, please let me know.

55 J K Galbraith, *The Economics of Innocent Fraud* (Penguin, 2004)

Al Dunlap vs Sunbeam

56 The title of the best book on Dunlap's career, from a journalist who followed it on the way up, and all the way down. John Byrn, *Chainsaw: The notorious career of Al Dunlap in the era of profit-at-any-price* (HarperBusiness, 1999)

57 http://www.portfolio.com/executives/2009/04/22/Al-Dunlap-Profile

58 'How Al Dunlap self-destructed', *Business Week*, 6 July 1998

Bear Stearns

59 http://dealbreaker.com/tag/bear-stearns/

60 'Bear CEO's handling of crisis raises issues', *Wall Street Journal*, 1 November 2007

61 'Bringing Down Bear Stearns', August 2008, is superbly written, though controversial – as it suggests that Bear Stearns was brought down in a coordinated attack by speculators.

62 The article was by Gretchen Morgenson, called 'Rescue me – Fed bailout crosses a line'.

63 The collapse of the fictional bank in the Oliver Stone movie *Wall Street: Money Never Sleeps* has a remarkable similarity to the story of Bear Stearns. So the first hour is recommended for anyone who wants to understand how the collapse came about, and what the consequences of it were. The second hour is certainly not.

Ratners

64 You can read the story in Ratner's own words: *The Rise and Fall… and Rise Again* (Capstone, 2007)

65 'Why diamonds are forever for Gerald Ratner', *Independent on Sunday*, 21 April 1991

Clarence Hatry

66 'Narcissistic Leaders: The incredible pros, the inevitable cons', *Harvard Business Review*, January–February 2000

67 *The Hatry Case: Eight current misconceptions* (C. Nicholls & Co., 1938).

Heads they win, tails we lose

68   David L Dotlich and Peter C Cairo: *Why CEOs Fail* (Jossey-Bass, 2003)

69   Stanley Milgram, *Obedience to Authority* (Taylor & Francis, 1974)

70   'Towards a political theory of leadership', A P Ammeter *et al*, *The Leadership Quarterly*, 2002

71   Danielle S Beu and M Ronald Buckley, 'This is war: How the politically astute achieve crimes of obedience through the use of moral disengagement', *The Leadership Quarterly*, 2004

72   'CEO involvement in the selection of new board members', *Journal of Finance*, October 1999

73   Executive Paywatch: http://www.aflcio.org/corporatewatch/paywatch/pay/index.cfm#_ftn1

74   Joseph Stiglitz, *The Roaring Nineties* (W.W. Norton, 2003)

Chapter Five

75   Dave Arnott: 'Corporate Cults: The insidious lure of the all-consuming organization' (AMACOM, 2000)

Iceland

76   'West Ham's Icelandic connection drawing to a close', *Daily Telegraph*, 9 January 2010

77   Michael Lewis wrote an unforgettable article about Iceland's collapse in Vanity Fair: 'Wall Street on the Tundra', *Vanity Fair*, April 2009. Or here: http://www.vanityfair.com/politics/features/2009/04/iceland200904

78   The content of the presentation fed into the paper 'The Icelandic banking crisis and what to do about it', CEPR Policy Insight No. 26. Download from http://www.cepr.org.

79   'Iceland: What ugly secrets are waiting to be exposed in the meltdown?' *Daily Telegraph*, 15 August 2009

80   'Tired of waiting, Icelanders gather to create a roadmap for the future', *Huffington Post*, 11 November 2009

The South Sea Company

81   The South Sea Company is also covered at length in MacKay's *Extraordinary Popular Delusions*.

General Motors

82   'GM stumps the Senators', *The Nation*, 29 November 1958

83   *HBS Working Knowledge*, 15 June 2009

Albania

84   The story is told in the magazine of the International Monetary Fund by Christopher Jarvis, an employee who was there at the time: 'The rise and fall of Albania's pyramid schemes', *Finance and Development*, March 2000

85   The story of Vehbi Alimucaj was covered in 'Life as an Albanian Ponzi Scheme mogul', Radio Free Europe, 6 June 2000. Transcript here: http://www.nettime.org/Lists-Archives/nettime-l-0006/msg00030.html.

MRDA

86   Note this is, as usual in these cases, not exactly what was said in court. The correct quote is 'Well he would, wouldn't he' – which, unless you know the question, doesn't make any sense, and so has been embellished.

87   'Missing the Clues', PBS, 26 February 2002

88   The full speech is available here: http://www.sec.gov/news/speech/spch042803whd.htm.

89   'Enron's alchemy turns to lead for bankers', *Financial Times*, 28 February 2002

90   You can find more detail on how Enron attempted (with great success) to manipulate analysts in Loren Fox's 2002 book *Enron: The rise and fall* (Wiley).

91   'Ratings downgrade', James Surowiecki, *New Yorker*, 28 September 2009

92   'The ratings game', Kia Dennis, *University of Miami Law Review*, July 2009

Chapter Six

Lehman Brothers

93   Find it at http://www.kansascityfed.org/publicat/sympos/2005/pdf/rajan2005.pdf.

94   Quotes in this section from the BBC documentary *Our World*.

The Tulip Mania

95   The most popular source for the story of the Tulip Mania, like the Mississippi Scheme and The South Sea Bubble, is Mackay – but, as mentioned in the text, its veracity is in doubt.

96   Peter M Garber: *Famous First Bubbles: The fundamentals of early manias* (MIT Press, 2000)

97   Earl A Thompson: 'The Tulipmania: Fact or Artifact?' *Public Choice*, 2007

Charles Ponzi

98   Ponzi's story is well known, but is especially well told in *Ponzi Schemes, Invaders from Mars and More Impossible Delusions* by Joseph Bulgatz (Harmony, 1992).

Home-Stake Production Co

99   If you don't know this book, it is an elegant explanation of how the stock market works. It is still as relevant today as it was when it was published in 1976, even if the markets have changed.

100   A feature on the collapse, which names all the celebrity investors, was published in *Time* Magazine, 8 July 1974: 'Gulling the beautiful people'. You can find it in Time's online archive at http://www.time.com/

Boys will be boys

101   More on this in *The (Mis)behavior of Markets*, by Benoit Mandelbrot (Profile, 2004).

102   http://www.marcusevansassets.com/doc/press/Mappingthemindofmoneymakers_7.pdf

103   'Lehman bankruptcy report reveals misleading accounting tactics', *Inside Counsel Magazine*, May 2010

Chapter Seven

104   *The Effects of Mergers and Post-Merger Integration: A review of business consulting literature*, Paul Butler, draft mimeo, Bureau of Economics, Federal Trade Commission

AOL Time Warner

105   An in-depth investigation of what occurred along the way is in Alec Klein's *Stealing Time: Steve Case, Jerry Levin, and the collapse of AOL Time Warner* (Simon & Schuster, 2003).

106   An analysis from the time is available in a Harvard Business School paper 'Valuing the AOL Time Warner Merger' from 5 February 2002, which

combined public research sources, all of which turned out to be
spectacularly incorrect.

Royal Bank of Scotland and ABN Amro

107 'Fred the Shred and his love for a deal', *The Guardian*, 18 April 2008

Bank of Scotland and Halifax

108 'Halifax swallows the pride of Scotland', *Sunday Telegraph*, 6 May 2001

109 'Mortgage customers "urged to lie"': BBC *Money Programme*, 29 October 2003

110 'The Choice', BBC Radio 4, 3 November 2009

111 Evidence to the Treasury Select Committee, 10 February 2009

112 Read the full text of Paul Moore's statement to the Treasury Select
Committee here: http://bit.ly/eC6Igf.

USWeb

113 'Paying the price', Mark Gimein, *Industry Standard*, May 1998

114 'CEO quits job over UFO views', *San Francisco Chronicle*, 9 January 1999

When mergers go bad

115 http://www.mckinseyquarterly.com/Why_mergers_fail_1113

116 'Not All M&As are alike', Joseph Bower, *Harvard Business Review*,
March 2001

117 For more discussion, Richard Thaler, 'The winner's curse', *Journal of
Economic Perspectives* 2(1) (1988).

118 'Robert Campeau's special genius', *New York Times*, 17 January 1990

119 Hitt, King, Krishnana, Makri, Schijven, Shimizu, Zhu: *Mergers and
Acquisitions: Overcoming pitfalls, building synergy and creating value* (Business
Horizons 52, Kelley School of Business Indiana University, 2009, pp523–29)

Chapter Eight

AIG

120 http://gawker.com/5175745/aig-corporate-securitys-tips-for-surviving-an-
angry-mob

121 'AIG execs in Europe resist returning bonuses', Reuters, 25 March 2009

122 His story is told in depth in 'The man with the trillion dollar price on his head', *Sunday Times*, 17 May 2009.

123 NBC, 'The Tonight Show With Jay Leno,' 20 March 2009

Long Term Capital Management

124 The background to LTCM, and an explanation of the (albeit incomplete) genius of the insights that they had into risk, derivatives and trading, is covered excellently in two books on LTCM, *Inventing Money* (Nick Dunbar, Wiley & Sons, 2000) and *When Genius Failed: The rise and fall of Long-Term Capital Management* (Roger Lowenstein, Random House, 2000).

125 Nassim Nicholas Taleb has written two books, broadly on this subject: *Fooled by Randomness* (Penguin, 2004) and *The Black Swan* (Penguin, 2007). Or you can read the profile of Taleb written by Malcolm Gladwell in the *New Yorker*, which explains the same ideas: 'Blowing Up', http://www.gladwell.com/2002/2002_04_29_a_blowingup.htm

Letsbuyit.com

126 'Letsbuyit boardroom bickering to blame for collapse', *The Register*, 19 January 2001

127 'Kimble/Schmitz charged with embezzlement', *The Register*, 10 November 2003

Digiscents

128 The press release is preserved here: http://www.prnewswire.co.uk/cgi/news/release?id=61842.

129 http://www.chaddickerson.com/

Segway

130 The story behind Segway is covered in full by a journalist who was embedded behind the scenes before the launch. *Code Name Ginger: The Story Behind Segway and Dean Kamen's Quest to Invent a New World* (Steve Kemper, Harvard Business School Press, 2003)

131 '"Ginger": Kamen's Stirling Idea', *Wired*, 15 January 2001

132 'Reinventing the wheel', *Time* Magazine, 2 December 2001

Index